LOW-FAT
WAYS TO COOK
SALADS &
SIDE DISHES

LOW-FAT
WAYS TO COOK
SALADS &
SIDE DISHES

COMPILED AND EDITED BY
SUSAN M. MCINTOSH, M.S., R.D.

Oxmoor
House®

Library of Congress Catalog Number: 98-68285
ISBN: 0-8487-2210-8
Manufactured in the United States of America
First Printing 1999

Editor-in-Chief: Nancy Fitzpatrick Wyatt
Editorial Director, Special Interest Publications: Ann H. Harvey
Senior Foods Editor: Katherine M. Eakin
Senior Editor, Editorial Services: Olivia Kindig Wells
Art Director: James Boone

LOW-FAT WAYS TO COOK SALADS & SIDE DISHES

Menu and Recipe Consultant: Susan McEwen McIntosh, M.S., R.D.
Assistant Editor: Kelly Hooper Troiano
Associate Foods Editor: Anne Chappell Cain, M.S., M.P.H., R.D.
Copy Editor: Keri Bradford Anderson
Editorial Assistants: Suzanne Powell, Leslie P. Wells
Indexer: Mary Ann Laurens
Associate Art Director: Cynthia R. Cooper
Designer: Carol Damsky
Senior Photographer: Jim Bathie
Photographers: Howard L. Puckett, *Cooking Light* magazine;
  Ralph Anderson
Senior Photo Stylist: Kay E. Clarke
Photo Stylists: Cindy Manning Barr, *Cooking Light* magazine;
  Virginia R. Cravens
Director, Production and Distribution: Phillip Lee
Associate Production Manager: Vanessa Cobbs Richardson
Production Assistant: Faye Porter Bonner

Our appreciation to the staff of *Cooking Light* magazine and to the Southern
Progress Corporation library staff for their contributions to this book.

Cover: *Pasta Primavera (recipe on page 107)*
Frontispiece: *Basil-Wrapped Corn on the Cob (recipe on page 117)*

We're Here for You!

We at Oxmoor House are
dedicated to serving you with
reliable information that expands
your imagination and enriches your
life. We welcome your comments
and suggestions. Please write us at:

Oxmoor House, Inc.
Editor, *Low-Fat Ways To Cook
Salads & Side Dishes*
2100 Lakeshore Drive
Birmingham, AL 35209

CONTENTS

MAXIMIZE YOUR SALADS & SIDE DISHES

*S*alads and side dishes offer abundant options for healthy eating. Their basic ingredients—fruit, vegetables, and grains—are naturally low in fat and good sources of vitamins, minerals, and fiber. Read on to learn how to make the most of these dishes in preparing delicious, low-fat meals for family and guests.

Side dishes and salads boast some of the most important nutrients on the dinner table. And their major ingredients of fruit, vegetables, and grains have unique colors, textures, and flavors that are unsurpassed by other foods.

This book is packed with high-flavor salads, including Pesto Potato Salad, Creamy Macaroni Salad, and Stuffed Pear Salad. You'll also find meal-size salads such as Grilled Chicken Caesar Salad and Layered Nacho Salad.

Side dishes range from simple Honeyed Bananas to more elaborate Grilled Vegetables with Balsamic Vinaigrette and Polenta with Wild Mushroom Sauce.

The final chapter includes low-fat versions of classic dressings such as Caesar Salad Dressing as well as innovative recipes like Cool Pineapple Dressing. Several bold salsa recipes offer a different way to enjoy fruit and vegetables.

Before you make your shopping list for any of these salads, side dishes, or salsas, read the next few pages. You will learn the best ways to select, store, and prepare fruit, vegetables, and grains.

FABULOUS FRUIT

Health experts recommend that we eat two to four servings of fruit daily. A serving includes one medium piece of fruit; ¾ cup juice; ½ cup berries or cut fruit; ½ cup canned, frozen, or cooked fruit; or ¼ cup dried fruit. At least one of these servings should be rich in vitamin C. (Citrus fruit, berries, and melon are good sources of vitamin C.)

When you shop for fruit, look beyond the usual red apple. Try new varieties of apples and pears, such as Gala and Newtown Pippin apples and Bosc and Anjou pears. Or be a bit bolder and select tropical fruit like mangoes, papayas, starfruit, and guava to add excitement to meals and snacks.

Many fruit lovers keep a supply of dried fruit on hand for those days when the bowl of apples and bananas runs low. Raisins, prunes, dried apple slices, and dried mixed fruit are convenient for snacks and brown bag lunches. Also, keep canned and frozen fruit on hand to ensure that fruit is always available.

Today's supermarkets and produce stands offer a huge selection of fresh fruit throughout the year.

STORAGE

Place most fruit in plastic bags, and refrigerate until needed. Here are some other guidelines.

•Allow unripe bananas to ripen at room temperature; then place the ripe bananas in the refrigerator to stop further ripening. The peel will turn brown, but the flesh remains edible.

•Treat unripe peaches, pears, mangoes, and papayas as you would bananas—leave them at room temperature until ripened. Enjoy the ripened fruit or place it in the refrigerator for two or three days.

•Speed up the ripening of unripe bananas, peaches, pears, and mangoes by placing the fruit in a paper bag at room temperature.

•Do not wash berries until you are ready to use them. It is usually best to store berries in a single layer on a paper towel in a moisture-proof container in the refrigerator for only one to three days.

•Keep a whole watermelon in the refrigerator up to one week; store cut watermelon for one to two days. Store unripe honeydew and cantaloupe at room temperature. Wrap ripe cantaloupe and honeydew melons in plastic wrap (since they can absorb other odors), and store them in the refrigerator.

•Pineapple must ripen on the plant to achieve maximum sweetness. Ideally, you should purchase a slightly soft, ripe pineapple, wrap it in plastic, and store it in the refrigerator for no more than three days. Slightly unripe pineapple will become less acidic (but not sweeter) if kept at room temperature for a few days.

SELECTION

For the freshest and most economical selections, choose fruit that is in season and grown locally. Thanks to modern transportation, you can also enjoy fruit from other parts of the world, although it is often more expensive than domestic varieties.

When purchasing fresh fruit, evaluate its quality by ripeness, texture, aroma, and color. Stay away from fruit that shows any sign of bumps or bruises. Bruising hastens spoilage, so handle fresh fruit gently when shopping. Whenever possible, choose loose fruit rather than packaged; then you will be able to inspect each piece.

Ask that fruit be bagged separately so that it will not be damaged by heavy cans or boxes.

PREPARATION

Fruit requires little preparation, and it is often best in its simplest form. Here are some principles to remember.

•Wash all fresh fruit under cold running water, using a vegetable brush when possible. Soap may leave a residue on the fruit after rinsing and is not recommended.

•To get the most fiber from fruit, leave on the peel. For example, an apple with the peel contains about 3 grams fiber, while a peeled apple has 2.4 grams.

•Avoid overcooking fruit side dishes since the cooking process decreases fiber as well as vitamins.

Eat a variety of vegetables to obtain a broad spectrum of vitamins and minerals. Their flavors, colors, and textures also add interest to menus.

VERSATILE VEGETABLES

Vegetable salads and side dishes have much to offer any meal. Most are simple to prepare, and they are unmatched in the amounts of complex carbohydrates, fiber, vitamins, and minerals they contain. Vegetables also have little or no fat and cholesterol unless other ingredients are added during preparation.

Vegetables provide a great variety of vitamins and minerals. Deep yellow and dark green leafy vegetables are especially high in beta carotene (which forms vitamin A). These healthy vegetables include carrots, sweet potatoes, spinach, broccoli, and kale. Vitamin C is found in green peppers, broccoli, tomatoes, and potatoes. Dark green leafy vegetables supply folic acid.

While other vegetables, such as lima beans and English peas, are not good sources of specific vitamins, they are rich in complex carbohydrates. And almost all vegetables provide fiber—especially dried beans and peas.

It is important to eat a variety of vegetables since they supply varying amounts and types of nutrients. Nutritionists recommend three to five servings of vegetables daily. One serving is ½ cup chopped raw, nonleafy vegetables; 1 cup leafy, raw vegetables; ½ cup cooked vegetables; or ¾ cup vegetable juice.

SELECTION

Purchase fresh vegetables as close as possible to the time you plan to use them. The quality of the produce and the nutrient content decreases with each day of storage.

When selecting vegetables, look for freshness and crispness. Avoid vegetables that have soft or bruised spots. Often a bruised or bad spot on one item causes spoilage among the others.

Select fresh crisp salad greens that have firm, unblemished leaves and good color. Avoid greens that are oversized, limp, spotty, or yellow. Check the stem end for freshness; if it's brown, slimy, or dry, make another selection.

STORAGE

Store most fresh vegetables in plastic bags in the refrigerator. Refrigerated vegetables lose only one-fourth to one-third the amount of vitamin C that they would lose if left at room temperature. Place the vegetables in the drawers at the bottom of the refrigerator to prevent the moisture (and nutrient) loss that will more likely occur on the top shelves.

Green leafy vegetables wilt quickly and change flavor as the water evaporates from them. To prevent this, rinse them under cool water, and drain thoroughly. To remove excess moisture, use a salad spinner; dry the greens in small batches to avoid bruising the leaves. You can also place wet greens on a cotton towel; gather the ends of the towel, and shake gently to remove excess water.

Once you have washed and dried the greens, wrap them in paper towels, place in an airtight container, and chill. The paper towel pulls moisture away from the greens, and the airtight container keeps the moisture from evaporating.

The sweet taste of fresh corn, green beans, and peas diminishes with storage because their sugar turns to starch. Store them dry and unwashed in plastic bags in the refrigerator for only short periods of time.

Store onions, potatoes, and hard-rind vegetables such as winter squash in a cool, dry, dark place instead of the refrigerator. Do not store potatoes and onions together—the onions will absorb moisture from the potatoes, causing the onions to spoil faster.

PREPARATION

How you store and prepare fresh produce can help maintain its nutritional punch. Oxygen, light, and heat drain vital nutrients such as vitamins A and C. Here are some tips on how to keep those vitamins and minerals where they belong—in your vegetables.

•Eat fresh vegetables right away. Vitamins and minerals in fresh vegetables deteriorate faster than those in meats and fresh fruits. Vitamin C and the fat-soluble vitamins A, D, E, and K are all vulnerable. If you have to delay serving them, wrap the vegetables tightly in plastic before refrigerating.

•Wash all vegetables thoroughly with water and a vegetable brush; peel only if necessary. The peels on vegetables such as potatoes, cucumber, and zucchini are edible and contain significant amounts of fiber. In fact, the most vitamin C in a potato lies right beneath the skin.

•Avoid chopping too much. Lots of chopping exposes more surface area to oxygen, which destroys certain vitamins.

•Steam and stir-fry vegetables. These methods of cooking will preserve nutrients and retain much of the color and texture of fresh vegetables. Steaming and stir-frying are quick, and neither requires immersion in water (which leaches nutrients).

•If cooking in water, use as little as possible and avoid overcooking. When the vegetables are bright in color and crisp-tender, they are ready to eat.

•Cook vegetables in the microwave with little or no water to retain natural flavor and nutrients.

Legume Power

A staple food throughout the world, legumes (including black beans, black-eyed peas, and lentils) are loaded with protein. Legumes are also packed with complex carbohydrates, fiber, vitamins, and minerals. Throughout this book, you'll find several salads and side dishes featuring legumes.

Savvy Green Salads

Arugula, Watercress, Beet greens, Dandelion greens, Purple kale, Romaine lettuce, White kale, Red leaf lettuce, Radicchio, Boston lettuce

If iceberg lettuce immediately comes to mind when you think of salad greens, you may be in a salad rut. Use your imagination to mix different varieties of greens for great salad flavor. Combine tangy greens with those milder in flavor, crisp greens with tender varieties, and pale greens with those flashier in color.

For a bitter taste, use dandelion, turnip or collard greens; romaine; or radicchio. Beet greens taste like beets; kale flavor is similar to cabbage; watercress and arugula are peppery-flavored; and Boston lettuce is sweet and succulent.

GREAT GRAINS

Grains such as rice, bulgur, barley, and pasta are low-fat sources of complex carbohydrates that provide a variety of textures and flavors to low-fat meals. Whole-grain varieties are also good sources of fiber.

Don't shortchange yourself by using only the familiar white rice. Basmati rice and jasmine rice are two types of fragrant rices that tantalize the senses while cooking. Brown rice is crunchy and has a more pronounced nutty flavor than white. It is higher in fiber because of the bran layer present.

In addition to these varieties of rice, try unusual whole grains such as barley, buckwheat, bulgur, and quinoa. They will add fiber, vitamins, and several minerals to salads and side dishes.

Pastas are available in many shapes, sizes, flavors, and colors. As with rice and other grains, pasta has almost no fat; it is the rich sauce that adds the fat.

The Skinny on Sauces and Dressings

When butter, cheese, and heavy cream are added to foods like rice and pasta, they run up the calories, fat, and cholesterol. To avoid this, use creative recipes that call for herbs and other seasonings to boost flavor while keeping fat grams low.

Salad dressings can also make the fat and calorie content soar in vegetable, fruit, and grain-based salads. Try one of the many healthy commercial dressings that are available, or make your own. Turn to pages 131–133 for ideas and recipes.

THE MAGIC OF HERBS AND SPICES

Use herbs and spices to liven up low-fat side dishes and salads.
This chart lists some natural matches.

Herb or Spice	Vegetables	Legumes, Pastas & Grains
Basil	asparagus, broccoli, cabbage, celery	beans, couscous, pasta, polenta, rice
Cardamom	pumpkin, squash, sweet potatoes	beans, bulgur, couscous, rice
Chili powder	corn, eggplant, tomatoes	beans, pasta, polenta, rice
Cinnamon	pumpkin, sweet potatoes, winter squash	bulgur, lentils, rice
Cloves	beets, green beans, onions, winter squash	beans, polenta
Cumin	cabbage, pumpkin, tomatoes	beans, lentils, rice
Curry powder	carrots, cauliflower, parsnips, potatoes, turnips	black beans, lentils, noodles, rice
Ginger	cabbage, carrots, squash, sweet potatoes	lentils, polenta, rice
Mustard	cabbage, coleslaw, cucumbers, green beans	beans, polenta
Oregano	broccoli, cabbage, corn, cucumbers, mushrooms	beans, lentils, pasta
Rosemary	green beans, peas, potatoes, spinach, turnips	bulgur, couscous, lentils, polenta, rice
Sage	eggplant, onions, tomatoes, winter squash	bulgur, polenta, rice, stuffings

LOW-FAT BASICS

*W*hether you are trying to lose or maintain weight, low-fat eating makes good sense. Research studies show that decreasing your fat intake reduces risks of heart disease, diabetes, and some types of cancer. The goal recommended by major health groups is an intake of 30 percent or less of total daily calories.

The *Low-Fat Ways To Cook* series gives you practical, delicious recipes with realistic advice about low-fat cooking and eating. The recipes are lower in total fat than traditional recipes. In fact, most provide less than 30 percent from fat and less than 10 percent from saturated fat.

In some recipes, the percentages can be deceiving. In fact, many of these salads and side dishes may be low in total fat grams and yet have greater than 30 percent of their calories from fat. For example, Nutty Asparagus on page 112 has only 44 calories per serving with 55 percent of these from fat. However, the total amount of fat is still only 2.7 grams, making this recipe—and others like it—a healthy choice.

If you do include a high-fat item during the day, you can balance it with low-fat choices for the rest of the day and still remain within the recommended guidelines. What's important is that your total fat intake over the day makes up less than 30 percent of the total calories. The goal of fat reduction is not to eliminate fat entirely. In fact, a small amount of fat is needed to transport fat-soluble vitamins and maintain other normal body functions.

FIGURING THE FAT

The easiest way to achieve a diet with 30 percent or fewer of total calories from fat is to establish a daily "fat budget" based on the total number of calories you need each day. Multiply your current weight by 15 to estimate your daily calorie requirements. Remember that calorie requirements vary according to age, body size, and level of activity. To gain or lose 1 pound a week, add or subtract 500 calories a day. (A diet of fewer than 1,200 calories is not recommended unless medically supervised.)

To calculate your recommended fat allowance, multiply your daily calorie needs by .30 and divide

DAILY FAT LIMITS		
Calories Per Day	30 Percent of Calories	Grams of Fat
1,200	360	40
1,500	450	50
1,800	540	60
2,000	600	67
2,200	660	73
2,500	750	83
2,800	840	93

by 9 (the number of calories in each gram of fat). You daily fat gram intake should not exceed this number. For quick reference, see the Daily Fat Limits chart above.

NUTRITIONAL ANALYSIS

Each recipe in *Low-Fat Ways To Cook Salads and Side Dishes* has been kitchen-tested by a staff of food professionals. In addition, registered dietitians have determined the nutrient information using a computer system that analyzes every ingredient. These efforts ensure the success of the recipes and will help you fit them into your own meal planning.

The nutrient grid that follows each recipe provides calories per serving and the percentage of calories from fat. The grid also lists the grams of total fat, saturated fat, protein, and carbohydrate, and the milligrams of cholesterol and sodium per serving. The nutrient values are as accurate as possible and are based on the following assumptions:

• When a recipe calls for cooked pasta or rice, we base the analysis on cooking without salt or fat.

• The calculations indicate that meat and poultry are trimmed of fat and skin before cooking.

• Only the amount of marinade absorbed by the food is calculated.

• Garnishes and other optional ingredients are not calculated.

• When a range is given for an ingredient (3 to 3½ cups, for instance), the lesser amount is calculated.

• Fruit and vegetables are unpeeled unless specified.

Gingered Tenderloin Salad (recipe on page 16)

MAIN-DISH SALADS

*T*oday's main-dish salads are popular offerings on lunch and supper menus everywhere. And these salad entrées are no longer simply mixtures of chicken and mayonnaise over lettuce leaves; instead, they feature steak, pork tenderloin, and even lobster.

Turn the page for hearty meat salad recipes such as Steak and Black-Eyed Pea Salad (page 14) and Asian Pork Salad (page 15). Updated versions of chicken salad start on page 16 and include bold-flavored Blackened Chicken Salad and Grilled Chicken Caesar Salad (page 18). Cobb Salad with a Twist (page 21) is the first of several delicious seafood salads. Layered Nacho Salad and other meatless main-dish salads follow on pages 30 and 31.

Pair any of these main-dish salads with crusty bread and perhaps a fruit side dish to create a satisfying, healthy lunch or supper.

Thai Barbecue Beef Salad

2 tablespoons fish sauce
2 cloves garlic
1 jalapeño pepper, seeded
1 tablespoon brown sugar
3 tablespoons fresh lime juice
1 tablespoon lime zest
1 tablespoon chile pepper oil
½ cup lightly packed fresh mint, chopped
¼ cup chopped green onions
1½ teaspoons peeled, grated gingerroot
4 shallots, thinly sliced lengthwise
1 pound sirloin steak (1½ inches thick)
½ teaspoon freshly ground pepper
¼ teaspoon salt
Vegetable cooking spray
8 cups mixed salad greens
3 tablespoons chopped fresh cilantro
½ cup diced sweet red pepper

Combine first 3 ingredients in container of an electric blender; cover and process until smooth. Add sugar and lime juice; cover and process until smooth. Stir in lime zest.

Divide mixture in half. Stir oil into 1 portion of sauce mixture; set aside. Add mint and next 3 ingredients to remaining half of sauce mixture; set aside.

Sprinkle steak evenly with ground pepper and salt. Coat grill rack with cooking spray; place on grill over medium-hot coals (350° to 400°). Place steak on rack; grill, covered, 8 minutes on each side or to desired degree of doneness. Remove steak from grill; let stand 5 minutes. Slice steak diagonally across grain into ¼-inch-thick slices; cut slices into ¼-inch-thick strips. Combine steak strips and mint mixture; cover and chill thoroughly.

Combine mixed greens and oil mixture; toss well. Arrange evenly on individual salad plates; top evenly with steak strip mixture. Sprinkle with cilantro and red pepper. Yield: 6 servings.

PER SERVING: 161 CALORIES (32% FROM FAT)
FAT 5.7G (SATURATED FAT 1.9G)
PROTEIN 20.2G CARBOHYDRATE 7.2G
CHOLESTEROL 55MG SODIUM 527MG

Steak and Black-Eyed Pea Salad

1 (12-ounce) lean flank steak
1 tablespoon spicy brown mustard
½ teaspoon garlic powder
¼ teaspoon pepper
Vegetable cooking spray
5 cups torn romaine lettuce
1 cup cherry tomatoes, halved
1 cup (¼-inch-thick) sliced cucumber
½ cup sliced onion, separated into rings
1 (15.8-ounce) can black-eyed peas, rinsed and drained
¾ cup fat-free Italian dressing

Trim fat from steak. Combine mustard, garlic powder, and pepper; spread over both sides of steak. Place steak on a broiler pan coated with cooking spray. Broil 5½ inches from heat (with electric oven door partially opened) 5 minutes on each side or until desired degree of doneness. Cut steak diagonally across grain into thin slices.

Combine steak, lettuce, and next 4 ingredients in a bowl. Drizzle dressing over salad, and toss well. Yield: 4 (2-cup) servings.

PER SERVING: 323 CALORIES (34% FROM FAT)
FAT 12.1G (SATURATED FAT 4.3G)
PROTEIN 24.6G CARBOHYDRATE 29.1G
CHOLESTEROL 45MG SODIUM 679MG

Steak and Black-Eyed Pea Salad

Asian Pork Salad

ASIAN PORK SALAD

¾ cup unsweetened orange juice, divided
¼ cup low-sodium teriyaki sauce, divided
1 tablespoon rice vinegar
1 tablespoon mirin (sweet rice wine)
2 teaspoons hoisin sauce
1 teaspoon sesame oil
1 clove garlic, minced
3 tablespoons brown sugar
2 tablespoons bourbon
¼ teaspoon dried crushed red pepper
1 (1-pound) pork tenderloin
Vegetable cooking spray
8 cups gourmet salad greens
½ cup sliced purple onion, separated into
    rings
1 (11-ounce) can mandarin oranges in light
    syrup, drained
1 (8-ounce) can sliced water chestnuts,
    drained
1 large sweet red pepper, sliced into rings
2 tablespoons sesame seeds, toasted

Combine ½ cup plus 2 tablespoons orange juice, 2 tablespoons teriyaki sauce, and next 5 ingredients in a small bowl; stir well. Cover and chill.

Combine remaining 2 tablespoons orange juice, remaining 2 tablespoons teriyaki sauce, brown sugar, bourbon, and crushed red pepper in a heavy-duty, zip-top plastic bag. Trim fat from pork; slice pork into 3- x ½-inch-wide strips. Add pork to bag. Seal; toss to coat. Marinate in refrigerator 15 minutes.

Place a large nonstick skillet coated with cooking spray over medium-high heat until hot. Add pork and marinade; cook 8 minutes or until pork is done and liquid almost evaporates. Remove from heat.

Arrange greens and next 4 ingredients on individual salad plates. Top each with 1 cup pork mixture; drizzle ¼ cup orange juice mixture over each salad. Sprinkle with sesame seeds. Yield: 4 servings.

PER SERVING: 322 CALORIES (19% FROM FAT)
FAT 6.8G (SATURATED FAT 1.5G)
PROTEIN 28.0G   CARBOHYDRATE 37.3G
CHOLESTEROL 74MG   SODIUM 382MG

GINGERED TENDERLOIN SALAD

(pictured on page 12)

½ cup ginger preserves
⅓ cup rice vinegar
⅓ cup low-sodium soy sauce
1½ tablespoons dark sesame oil
1 (1-pound) pork tenderloin
Vegetable cooking spray
6 cups shredded napa cabbage or other
   Chinese cabbage
1 cup thinly sliced sweet red pepper

Combine first 4 ingredients in a small saucepan. Place over medium heat; bring to a boil, stirring constantly. Remove from heat; cool completely.

Trim fat from pork. Place pork in a large heavy-duty, zip-top plastic bag. Pour half of soy sauce mixture over pork; reserve remaining half of soy sauce mixture. Seal bag, and shake until pork is well coated. Marinate in refrigerator at least 2 hours, turning bag occasionally.

Remove pork from marinade, reserving marinade. Place marinade in a small saucepan. Bring to a boil; remove from heat, and set aside. Coat grill rack with cooking spray; place on grill over medium-hot coals (350° to 400°). Insert a meat thermometer into thickest part of pork, if desired.

Place pork on rack; grill, covered, 20 minutes or until meat thermometer registers 160°, turning and basting occasionally with reserved marinade. Let pork stand 10 minutes; slice diagonally across grain into thin slices.

Combine cabbage and red pepper. Pour remaining half of soy sauce mixture over cabbage mixture; toss lightly.

Spoon cabbage mixture evenly onto individual salad plates. Arrange pork slices over cabbage mixture. Yield: 4 servings.

Note: If ginger preserves are not available, combine ½ cup low-sugar orange marmalade and 1½ tablespoons minced fresh gingerroot.

PER SERVING: 252 CALORIES (22% FROM FAT)
FAT 6.1G (SATURATED FAT 1.7G)
PROTEIN 25.8G   CARBOHYDRATE 24.0G
CHOLESTEROL 79MG   SODIUM 269MG

BLACKENED CHICKEN SALAD

Although this recipe calls for a homemade spice mix for blackening the chicken, there are several commercial mixes available. But be aware that they are often high in sodium.

3 cups chopped tomato
¾ cup diced sweet yellow pepper
¼ cup finely chopped purple onion
1 tablespoon sugar
3 tablespoons cider vinegar
¼ teaspoon salt
⅛ teaspoon pepper
¼ cup lemon juice
¼ cup Dijon mustard
3 tablespoons water
1 tablespoon honey
4 (4-ounce) skinned, boned chicken breast
   halves
3 tablespoons Spicy Seasoning
Vegetable cooking spray
1 pound Sugar Snap peas, trimmed
8 cups torn romaine lettuce
Flat-leaf parsley sprigs (optional)

Combine first 7 ingredients in a bowl, and toss well. Cover and chill.

Combine lemon juice and next 3 ingredients in a large bowl; stir well with a wire whisk. Cover mixture, and chill.

Rub chicken with Spicy Seasoning. Coat a large heavy skillet with cooking spray, and place over medium-high heat until hot.

Add chicken, and cook 7 minutes on each side or until chicken is done. Remove chicken from skillet, and cool. Cut chicken across grain into thin slices, and set aside.

Arrange peas in a steamer basket over boiling water. Cover and steam 2 minutes or until crisp-tender. Rinse under cold water; drain. Add peas and lettuce to lemon juice mixture; toss well.

Arrange lettuce mixture evenly in four large salad bowls; top each serving with 1 cup tomato mixture and 1 sliced chicken breast half. Garnish each serving with parsley sprigs, if desired. Yield: 4 servings.

Blackened Chicken Salad

SPICY SEASONING
2½ tablespoons paprika
2 tablespoons garlic powder
1 tablespoon salt
1 tablespoon onion powder
1 tablespoon dried thyme
1 tablespoon ground red pepper
1 tablespoon ground black pepper

Combine all ingredients. Store in an airtight container. Yield: about ½ cup.

PER SERVING: 298 CALORIES (16% FROM FAT)
FAT 5.4G (SATURATED FAT 1.0G)
PROTEIN 32.1G CARBOHYDRATE 31.0G
CHOLESTEROL 72MG SODIUM 1205MG

CURRIED CHICKEN SALAD PLATTER

1 fennel bulb (about 1 pound)
1 pound skinned, boned chicken breast halves
1 cup canned no-salt-added chicken broth
¼ cup dry white wine
½ cup nonfat mayonnaise
¼ cup nonfat sour cream
¼ cup plain nonfat yogurt
1 tablespoon minced onion
1 teaspoon curry powder
⅛ teaspoon salt
1 clove garlic, minced
Bibb lettuce leaves (optional)
1 cup sliced banana
1 cup peeled, sliced kiwifruit
1 cup sliced fresh strawberries
4 (1-inch-thick) slices cantaloupe

Trim tough stalks from fennel. Cut bulb in half lengthwise; remove core. Combine fennel, chicken, broth, and wine in a Dutch oven; bring to a boil. Cover, reduce heat, and simmer 15 minutes or until chicken is done. Remove chicken from broth, discarding fennel and broth. Cut chicken into ½-inch cubes. Cover and chill.

Combine mayonnaise and next 6 ingredients, stirring well. Add chicken; stir well.

Spoon chicken mixture evenly onto individual lettuce-lined salad plates, if desired. Arrange fruit evenly around chicken mixture. Yield: 4 servings.

PER SERVING: 296 CALORIES (12% FROM FAT)
FAT 4.0G (SATURATED FAT 1.2G)
PROTEIN 30.5G   CARBOHYDRATE 34.9G
CHOLESTEROL 73MG   SODIUM 550MG

GRILLED CHICKEN CAESAR SALAD

Toast the leftover French bread to make extra croutons for salads. Store croutons in a zip-top plastic bag.

4 (4-ounce) skinned, boned chicken breast halves
½ cup reduced-fat Caesar dressing, divided
2 cups cubed French bread
Olive oil-flavored vegetable cooking spray
6 cups torn romaine lettuce
1 cup sliced cucumber
2 medium tomatoes, each cut into 8 wedges
2 tablespoons freshly grated Parmesan cheese
Freshly ground pepper (optional)

Place chicken in a heavy-duty, zip-top plastic bag; pour ¼ cup dressing over chicken. Seal bag, and shake until chicken is well coated. Marinate in refrigerator 1 hour, turning bag once.

Coat bread cubes with cooking spray; place in a single layer on a baking sheet. Bake at 350° for 10 minutes or until croutons are lightly browned.

Remove chicken from marinade, discarding marinade. Coat grill rack with cooking spray; place on grill over medium-hot coals (350° to 400°). Place chicken on rack; grill, covered, 5 minutes on each side or until done. Cool slightly. Cut chicken crosswise into ¼-inch-thick slices.

Combine chicken, croutons, lettuce, and next 3 ingredients in a large serving bowl. Pour remaining ¼ cup dressing over lettuce mixture; toss well. Sprinkle with freshly ground pepper, if desired. Serve immediately. Yield: 6 (2-cup) servings.

PER SERVING: 206 CALORIES (31% FROM FAT)
FAT 7.2G (SATURATED FAT 1.3G)
PROTEIN 20.5G   CARBOHYDRATE 13.0G
CHOLESTEROL 53MG   SODIUM 554MG

Grilled Chicken Caesar Salad

PROVENÇALE PEPPER-CHICKEN SALAD

4 (4-ounce) skinned, boned chicken breast
  halves
1 teaspoon dried herbes de Provence
¼ teaspoon salt
¼ teaspoon pepper
2 cloves garlic, minced
Olive oil-flavored vegetable cooking spray
¾ cup chopped green onions
1 (1- x ¼-inch) julienne-sliced green pepper
1 (1- x ¼-inch) julienne-sliced sweet red
  pepper
1 (1- x ¼-inch) julienne-sliced sweet yellow
  pepper
¼ cup sun-dried tomato sprinkles (packed
  without oil)
¼ cup balsamic vinegar
1 tablespoon extra-virgin olive oil
2 cloves garlic, minced
6 cups gourmet salad greens
¼ cup niçoise olives

Place each chicken breast half between two sheets of heavy-duty plastic wrap. Flatten each to ½-inch thickness, using a meat mallet or rolling pin. Combine herbes de Provence and next 3 ingredients; rub mixture over both sides of chicken. Place a nonstick skillet coated with cooking spray over medium-high heat until hot. Add chicken; cook 3 minutes on each side or until done. Remove from skillet. Coat skillet with cooking spray. Add onions and sliced peppers; sauté 5 minutes.

Combine tomato sprinkles and next 3 ingredients; stir well. Arrange salad greens on individual salad plates; top each serving with a sliced chicken breast half and ½ cup pepper mixture. Drizzle 2 tablespoons vinegar mixture over each salad; top each serving with 1 tablespoon olives. Yield: 4 servings.

PER SERVING: 220 CALORIES (27% FROM FAT)
FAT 6.5G (SATURATED FAT 1.1G)
PROTEIN 29.5G   CARBOHYDRATE 11.5G
CHOLESTEROL 66MG   SODIUM 418MG

Provençale Pepper-Chicken Salad

COBB SALAD WITH A TWIST

¼ teaspoon minced fresh thyme
⅛ teaspoon pepper
½ pound halibut or other firm white fish fillet
Vegetable cooking spray
1½ cups sliced zucchini
1 cup sliced yellow squash
3 cups gourmet salad greens
½ cup diced tomato
2 tablespoons diced avocado
2 teaspoons olive oil
1 tablespoon white wine vinegar
1½ teaspoons honey
¼ teaspoon salt
¼ teaspoon minced fresh thyme
⅛ teaspoon pepper

Sprinkle ¼ teaspoon thyme and ⅛ teaspoon pepper over fish. Place fish on rack of a broiler pan coated with cooking spray. Broil 5½ inches from heat (with electric oven door partially opened) 4 minutes on each side or until fish flakes easily when tested with a fork. Cut fish into 1-inch chunks; set aside.

Combine zucchini and yellow squash in a 1-quart microwave-safe dish; cover with plastic wrap, and vent. Microwave at HIGH 3 minutes, stirring after 1 minute.

Arrange salad greens evenly on individual serving plates. Arrange squash mixture, tomato, and avocado in 3 rows over greens; top evenly with fish.

Combine oil and remaining 5 ingredients in a jar. Cover tightly, and shake vigorously. Drizzle dressing over salads. Yield: 2 servings.

PER SERVING: 247 CALORIES (35% FROM FAT)
FAT 9.5G (SATURATED FAT 1.3G)
PROTEIN 27.1G   CARBOHYDRATE 14.9G
CHOLESTEROL 53MG   SODIUM 369MG

PEPPERED HALIBUT, GREEN BEAN, AND OLIVE SALAD

¼ cup chopped fresh basil
¼ cup canned fat-free chicken broth
¼ cup balsamic vinegar
2 tablespoons water
2 teaspoons olive oil
½ teaspoon pepper
¼ teaspoon salt
2 cloves garlic, minced
½ pound green beans
4 (6-ounce) halibut steaks (about 1 inch thick)
Olive oil-flavored vegetable cooking spray
3 tablespoons freshly cracked mixed
   peppercorns
½ teaspoon salt
8 cups torn red leaf lettuce
2 tablespoons fresh lemon juice
2 medium tomatoes, each cut into 8 wedges
¼ cup chopped Greek ripe olives

Combine first 8 ingredients in a small bowl; cover and chill vinaigrette.

Wash beans; trim ends, and remove strings. Place beans in a large saucepan; add water to cover. Bring to a boil; boil 2 minutes. Rinse under cold water; drain well. Set aside.

Coat fish with cooking spray; rub both sides of fish evenly with peppercorns and ½ teaspoon salt. Coat grill rack with cooking spray; place on grill over medium-hot coals (350° to 400°). Place fish on rack; grill, uncovered, 5 minutes on each side or until fish flakes easily when tested with a fork. Remove from heat; cool slightly. Break fish into pieces; discard skin and bones.

Place lettuce in a bowl, and add lemon juice, tossing to coat. Arrange lettuce mixture evenly on individual salad plates. Top evenly with green beans, fish, tomato wedges, and olives. Drizzle vinaigrette evenly over salads. Yield: 4 servings.

PER SERVING: 274 CALORIES (26% FROM FAT)
FAT 7.8G (SATURATED FAT 1.1G)
PROTEIN 38.3G   CARBOHYDRATE 13.5G
CHOLESTEROL 80MG   SODIUM 620MG

Grilled Salmon Salad

GRILLED SALMON SALAD

*To make your own peppercorn
mustard, stir ½ teaspoon cracked pepper
into ¼ cup plus 1 tablespoon Dijon mustard.*

½ cup plus 1 tablespoon molasses, divided
¼ cup plus 1 tablespoon peppercorn mustard,
    divided
¼ cup plus 1 tablespoon malt vinegar, divided
6 (4-ounce) salmon fillets
2 large purple onions, sliced
Vegetable cooking spray
8 cups mixed baby salad greens
2 teaspoons vegetable oil
⅛ teaspoon salt

Combine ½ cup molasses, ¼ cup mustard, and 3
tablespoons vinegar, stirring well. Place fish and
onion in a shallow dish. Pour molasses mixture over
fish and onion. Cover and marinate in refrigerator 8
hours, turning occasionally.

Remove fish and onion from marinade, reserving
marinade. Place marinade in a small saucepan.
Bring to a boil; remove from heat.

Coat grill rack with cooking spray; place on grill
over medium-hot coals (350° to 400°). Place fish
and onion on rack; grill, covered, 4 minutes on
each side or until fish flakes easily when tested
with a fork and onion is tender, basting often with
reserved marinade.

Combine onion and greens. Combine remaining
1 tablespoon molasses, remaining 1 tablespoon
mustard, remaining 2 tablespoons vinegar, oil, and
salt; pour over greens mixture, and toss lightly.
Spoon evenly onto individual serving plates. Top
each serving with a fish fillet. Yield: 6 servings.

PER SERVING: 327 CALORIES (33% FROM FAT)
FAT 12.0G (SATURATED FAT 1.9G)
PROTEIN 24.4G   CARBOHYDRATE 29.2G
CHOLESTEROL 74MG   SODIUM 495MG

TUNA AND ARTICHOKE PASTA SALAD

2 teaspoons grated lemon rind
3 tablespoons fresh lemon juice
3 tablespoons extra-virgin olive oil
1 tablespoon peeled, minced gingerroot
2 cloves garlic, minced
4 cups hot cooked elbow macaroni (about 8
    ounces uncooked), cooked without salt
    or fat
1 cup cherry tomatoes, halved
½ cup chopped green onions
⅓ cup chopped fresh flat-leaf parsley
1 (6-ounce) can albacore tuna in water,
    drained and flaked
1 (14-ounce) can quartered artichoke hearts,
    drained

Combine first 5 ingredients in a large bowl. Add
pasta and remaining ingredients; toss gently to coat.
Cover; chill 1 hour. Yield: 8 (1-cup) servings.

PER SERVING: 185 CALORIES (29% FROM FAT)
FAT 6.0G (SATURATED FAT 0.9G)
PROTEIN 8.6G   CARBOHYDRATE 24.9G
CHOLESTEROL 6MG   SODIUM 91MG

FYI

Several varieties of tuna are on the grocery
shelf—white (albacore) or light, solid pack or
chunk, and tuna packed in water or oil.

White albacore tuna has a milder taste and
lighter color than light tuna and is the best
choice for main-dish salads. Tuna packed in
water is much lower in fat and calories than
tuna packed in oil, even if the oil has been
drained.

Salade Niçoise

SALADE NIÇOISE

3 tablespoons fresh lemon juice
2 (8-ounce) tuna steaks
Freshly ground pepper
Vegetable cooking spray
10 small round red potatoes (about
    1 pound), halved
½ pound green beans, trimmed
4 cups torn romaine lettuce
4 cups trimmed watercress (about 1 bunch)
3 medium tomatoes, each cut into 6 wedges
3 hard-cooked eggs, each quartered
    lengthwise
1 small green pepper, cut into strips
½ cup niçoise olives
2 tablespoons capers
6 canned anchovy fillets
Garlic-Basil Vinaigrette

Drizzle lemon juice over fish; sprinkle with ground pepper. Marinate in refrigerator 15 minutes; discard lemon juice.

Coat grill rack with cooking spray; place on grill over medium-hot coals (350° to 400°). Place fish on rack; grill, covered, 4 minutes on each side or until fish flakes easily when tested with a fork. Break fish into chunks; set aside.

Arrange potato in a steamer basket over boiling water. Cover and steam 3 minutes. Add green beans; cover and steam 8 additional minutes or until vegetables are crisp-tender. Cool.

Combine lettuce and watercress on a large serving platter. Arrange fish, potato, green beans, tomato, eggs, and pepper strips over greens. Top with olives, capers, and anchovies. Drizzle with Garlic-Basil Vinaigrette. Yield: 6 servings.

GARLIC-BASIL VINAIGRETTE

⅓ cup canned low-sodium chicken broth
1½ tablespoons chopped fresh basil
1 tablespoon extra-virgin olive oil
1 tablespoon fresh lemon juice
1 tablespoon red wine vinegar
1 teaspoon Dijon mustard
3 cloves garlic, halved
Freshly ground pepper

Combine all ingredients in container of an electric blender; cover and process until smooth. Yield: ¼ cup plus 2 tablespoons.

PER SERVING: 295 CALORIES (31% FROM FAT)
FAT 10.1G (SATURATED FAT 2.2G)
PROTEIN 30.0G CARBOHYDRATE 22.0G
CHOLESTEROL 64MG SODIUM 458MG

CRAB-PAPAYA SALAD

If papayas aren't available, substitute fresh cantaloupe wedges.

½ cup chopped sweet red pepper
⅓ cup reduced-fat mayonnaise
¼ cup chopped green onions
¼ cup mango chutney
1½ tablespoons horseradish mustard
¼ teaspoon freshly ground pepper
1 pound fresh lump crabmeat, drained
3 small papayas, peeled, cut in half lengthwise, and seeded
Green leaf lettuce leaves (optional)

Combine first 7 ingredients, stirring well. Cover and chill.

To serve, spoon ½ cup crab mixture into each papaya half. Place papaya halves on lettuce-lined salad plates, if desired. Yield: 6 servings.

PER SERVING: 202 CALORIES (23% FROM FAT)
FAT 5.2G (SATURATED FAT 0.8G)
PROTEIN 15.3G CARBOHYDRATE 23.2G
CHOLESTEROL 75MG SODIUM 478MG

MUSSEL SALAD WITH FENNEL

Diced fennel gives this salad a crunchy texture and a bold, aniselike flavor.

12 small round red potatoes (about 1½ pounds)
48 fresh mussels, scrubbed and debearded
1 (1-pound) fennel bulb with stalks
½ cup sherry vinegar
3 tablespoons diced purple onion
1 tablespoon finely chopped fresh tarragon
2 tablespoons olive oil
¾ teaspoon salt
¾ teaspoon pepper
3 cloves garlic, minced
2 medium tomatoes, cut into wedges
6 cups torn romaine lettuce
2 cup torn radicchio
2 hard-cooked eggs, each quartered lengthwise

Place potatoes in a saucepan; add water to cover. Bring to a boil. Cover, reduce heat, and simmer 15 minutes or until tender. Drain and set aside.

Steam mussels, covered, 10 minutes or until shells open; discard any unopened shells.

Trim tough outer leaves from fennel. Dice stalks to measure 1 cup; set aside. Cut fennel bulb in half vertically; discard core. Cut each half crosswise into thin slices to measure ½ cup, and set aside. Reserve remaining fennel for another use.

Combine vinegar and next 6 ingredients in a large bowl; stir well. Reserve ¼ cup dressing; set aside. Add potatoes, mussels, fennel, and tomato wedges to bowl; toss gently to coat. Cover and chill 30 minutes.

Combine reserved ¼ cup dressing, romaine lettuce, and radicchio in a bowl; toss well. Arrange greens evenly in individual salad bowls. Arrange mussel mixture and egg quarters evenly over salads. Yield: 4 servings.

PER SERVING: 405 CALORIES (28% FROM FAT)
FAT 12.5G (SATURATED FAT 2.2G)
PROTEIN 23.4G CARBOHYDRATE 44.9G
CHOLESTEROL 132MG SODIUM 944MG

LOBSTER-MANGO SALAD

In season from June through August, ripe mangoes have yellow to red flesh that tastes like a combination of peach and pineapple. A medium mango will yield about 1 cup of cubed or sliced fruit.

⅓ cup fresh orange juice
¼ cup fresh lime juice
2 teaspoons peeled, minced gingerroot
½ teaspoon salt
1 cup peeled, cubed mango
¾ cup minced purple onion
¼ cup seeded, finely chopped serrano chile
3 tablespoons chopped fresh mint
1 head Belgian endive (about ¼ pound)
2 (1½-pound) lobsters, cooked
8 cups gourmet salad greens
32 (9- x ½- x ⅛-inch) strips peeled jicama
24 asparagus spears, steamed and chilled
1 teaspoon freshly ground pepper

Combine first 4 ingredients; stir well. Combine 3 tablespoons juice mixture, mango, and next 3 ingredients; stir well. Set aside.

Separate endive into leaves, reserving 12 outer leaves. Thinly slice remaining leaves; set aside.

Remove meat from lobster tails and claws; set claw meat aside. Thinly slice tail meat; set aside.

Drizzle ⅓ cup juice mixture over salad greens, and toss gently to coat. Arrange greens evenly on individual salad plates.

Arrange 3 endive leaves, 8 jicama strips, and 6 asparagus spears on 1 side of each plate. Arrange claw meat on other side of each plate. Spoon ½ cup mango mixture onto center of each plate. Arrange tail slices, overlapping, on mango mixture. Drizzle remaining juice mixture evenly over lobster meat. Sprinkle pepper over salads, and top with sliced endive. Yield: 4 servings.

PER SERVING: 186 CALORIES (5% FROM FAT)
FAT 1.1G (SATURATED FAT 0.2G)
PROTEIN 19.5G CARBOHYDRATE 26.8G
CHOLESTEROL 54MG   SODIUM 595MG

Slicing Mangoes

The mango can be tricky to cut because it has a rather large seed that grows lengthwise inside the fruit. With a sharp knife, slice the fruit lengthwise on each side of the flat pit.

Holding the mango half in the palm of your hand, score the pulp in square cross-sections. Be sure to slice to, but not through, the skin.

Turn the mango inside out, and cut the chunks from the skin.

Lobster-Mango Salad

CITRUS-SEAFOOD SALAD

Add some crusty rolls and a glass of crisp white wine, and you have an elegant light meal.

1 pound unpeeled large fresh shrimp
1 cup water
½ cup dry white wine
¼ teaspoon dried thyme
¼ teaspoon dried marjoram
¾ pound bay scallops
½ cup thinly sliced purple onion, separated
     into rings
¼ teaspoon grated orange rind
¼ cup fresh orange juice
1 tablespoon fresh lemon juice
1 tablespoon olive oil
1 tablespoon Dijon mustard
¾ teaspoon sugar
¼ teaspoon pepper
⅛ teaspoon salt
6 cups small spinach leaves
2 cups orange sections
1 medium cucumber, peeled, cut in half
     lengthwise, and sliced

Peel shrimp; devein, if desired. Combine water and next 3 ingredients in a large skillet; bring to a boil. Add shrimp and scallops; cover, reduce heat, and simmer 4 minutes or until shrimp turn pink and scallops are opaque. Drain.

Combine shrimp, scallops, and onion in a large bowl. Combine orange rind and next 7 ingredients in a small bowl; stir well. Pour ¼ cup orange juice mixture over shrimp mixture; toss well. Cover and chill 30 minutes. Cover and chill remaining orange juice mixture.

Add spinach, orange sections, and cucumber to shrimp mixture; pour remaining orange juice mixture over salad. Toss well. Yield: 6 (2-cup) servings.

PER SERVING: 206 CALORIES (20% FROM FAT)
FAT 4.5G (SATURATED FAT 0.7G)
PROTEIN 27.3G CARBOHYDRATE 14.3G
CHOLESTEROL 134MG SODIUM 373MG

SHRIMP SALAD WITH TOMATO VINAIGRETTE

48 unpeeled large fresh shrimp (about 2 pounds)
4 (1-inch-thick) slices day-old French bread or
     other firm white bread, cut into 1-inch cubes
1 large tomato, cut into 1-inch-thick slices
1 teaspoon olive oil
¼ teaspoon salt
¼ teaspoon freshly ground pepper
3 tablespoons coarsely chopped fresh parsley
2 tablespoons fresh lemon juice
1 tablespoon olive oil
1 tablespoon canned chipotle chile in adobo sauce
1 tablespoon water
2 teaspoons ground coriander
¼ teaspoon salt
¼ teaspoon pepper
1 clove garlic, chopped
Vegetable cooking spray
9½ cups torn romaine lettuce
¾ cup peeled, cubed avocado
½ cup sliced purple onion

Peel shrimp; devein, if desired. Cover and chill.

Place bread in a single layer on a baking sheet. Bake at 350° for 12 minutes. Set croutons aside.

Brush tomato evenly with 1 teaspoon oil; sprinkle with ¼ teaspoon salt and ¼ teaspoon pepper. Place tomato on a baking sheet. Broil 5½ inches from heat (with electric oven door partially opened) 10 minutes on each side or until blackened.

Position knife blade in food processor bowl; add tomato, parsley, and next 8 ingredients. Process until blended. Divide vinaigrette in half. Set aside.

Thread shrimp onto six 12-inch skewers, and brush with half of vinaigrette. Coat grill rack with cooking spray; place on grill over medium-hot coals (350° to 400°). Grill shrimp, covered, 4 minutes on each side or until shrimp turn pink.

Combine remaining half of vinaigrette, croutons, shrimp, lettuce, avocado, and sliced onion in a large bowl; toss gently to coat. Yield: 6 (2½-cup) servings.

PER SERVING: 257 CALORIES (30% FROM FAT)
FAT 8.7G (SATURATED FAT 1.4G)
PROTEIN 27.0G CARBOHYDRATE 17.4G
CHOLESTEROL 173MG SODIUM 495MG

SHRIMP AND ORZO SALAD

You can prepare this recipe even more quickly if you use precooked shrimp.

⅓ cup red wine vinegar
1 teaspoon dried basil
1 teaspoon olive oil
½ teaspoon salt
½ teaspoon dried oregano
¼ teaspoon pepper
1 cup orzo, uncooked
2 cups seeded, diced tomato
1 cup frozen English peas, thawed
½ cup finely chopped purple onion
¼ cup chopped fresh parsley
1 pound unpeeled medium-size fresh shrimp,
    cooked and peeled
Boston lettuce leaves (optional)

Combine first 6 ingredients in a large bowl. Stir well; set aside.

Cook orzo according to package directions, omitting salt and fat. Drain well.

Add orzo, tomato, peas, chopped onion, parsley, and shrimp to vinegar mixture; toss well. Cover and chill. Serve salad in a lettuce-lined bowl, if desired. Yield: 4 (1½-cup) servings.

PER SERVING: 321 CALORIES (11% FROM FAT)
FAT 3.8G (SATURATED FAT 0.6G)
PROTEIN 26.0G   CARBOHYDRATE 45.1G
CHOLESTEROL 129MG   SODIUM 475MG

Shrimp and Orzo Salad

Layered Nacho Salad

LAYERED NACHO SALAD

6 (8-inch) corn tortillas
Vegetable cooking spray
⅓ cup chopped onion
2 (16-ounce) cans red kidney beans, drained
2 pickled jalapeño peppers, seeded and
     chopped
¼ cup water
1 small ripe avocado (about ½ pound), peeled
     and cut into chunks
½ cup seeded, chopped tomato
2 tablespoons chopped onion
2 tablespoons lime juice
¼ teaspoon salt
3 cups finely shredded romaine lettuce
¼ cup (1 ounce) finely shredded reduced-fat
     Cheddar cheese
3 radishes, thinly sliced
Southwestern Vinaigrette

Place tortillas on a baking sheet coated with cooking spray. Bake at 350° for 6 minutes; turn tortillas over. Bake 6 additional minutes or until crisp; cool.

Coat a saucepan with cooking spray; place over medium-high heat until hot. Add ⅓ cup onion; sauté until tender. Stir in kidney beans, jalapeño pepper, and water. Reduce heat; cook, uncovered, 15 minutes or until mixture becomes a thick paste, stirring occasionally and mashing beans with a spoon or fork. Set aside.

Place avocado in container of an electric blender; cover and process until smooth. Stir in tomato and next 3 ingredients.

Place 1 tortilla on each individual serving plate; top each with ½ cup lettuce. Spoon bean mixture over lettuce; top with avocado mixture. Sprinkle 2 teaspoons cheese over each salad; top with radish. Serve with Southwestern Vinaigrette. Yield: 6 servings.

SOUTHWESTERN VINAIGRETTE

½ cup no-salt-added mild salsa
2 tablespoons minced fresh cilantro
3 tablespoons lime juice
1 tablespoon white wine vinegar
1 tablespoon Dijon mustard
¼ teaspoon chili powder
¼ teaspoon pepper

Combine all ingredients in a bowl, stirring well. Cover and chill. Yield: ¾ cup plus 2 tablespoons.

PER SERVING: 188 CALORIES (30% FROM FAT)
FAT 6.2G (SATURATED FAT 1.2G)
PROTEIN 12.6G   CARBOHYDRATE 38.1G
CHOLESTEROL 3MG   SODIUM 300MG

COUSCOUS AND BLACK BEAN SALAD

1 large orange
⅛ teaspoon salt
⅔ cup couscous, uncooked
1 cup canned black beans, rinsed and drained
½ cup chopped sweet red pepper
¼ cup chopped green onions
2 tablespoons chopped fresh parsley
1 tablespoon seasoned rice vinegar
1½ teaspoons vegetable oil
¼ teaspoon ground cumin

Grate ¼ teaspoon orange rind, and set aside. Squeeze juice from orange over a bowl; reserve ¼ cup juice, and set aside. Add water to remaining juice in bowl to measure 1 cup.

Bring water mixture and salt to a boil in a saucepan; stir in couscous. Remove from heat; cover and let stand 5 minutes. Fluff with a fork. Cool slightly. Stir in orange rind, beans, and next 3 ingredients.

Combine reserved ¼ cup orange juice, vinegar, oil, and cumin. Add couscous mixture; toss well. Yield: 2 (2-cup) servings.

PER SERVING: 342 CALORIES (13% FROM FAT)
FAT 4.8G (SATURATED FAT 0.8G)
PROTEIN 14.7G   CARBOHYDRATE 62.5G
CHOLESTEROL 0MG   SODIUM 391MG

THREE-GREENS SALAD WITH GARBANZOS

4 cups cooked farfalle (bow tie pasta), cooked without salt or fat
4 cups trimmed arugula
2 cups thinly sliced radicchio
2 medium heads Belgian endive, quartered and thinly sliced lengthwise
1 (19-ounce) can garbanzo beans (chick-peas), drained
¼ cup plus 2 tablespoons balsamic vinegar
¼ cup canned low-sodium chicken broth
2 tablespoons extra-virgin olive oil
¼ cup finely chopped fresh flat-leaf parsley
2 ounces shaved fresh Parmesan cheese

Combine first 5 ingredients in a large bowl; toss well. Combine vinegar, broth, and oil; stir well with a wire whisk. Pour over pasta mixture; toss gently to coat. Sprinkle with parsley and cheese. Yield: 6 (2-cup) servings.

PER SERVING: 290 CALORIES (27% FROM FAT)
FAT 8.6G (SATURATED FAT 2.3G)
PROTEIN 12.0G   CARBOHYDRATE 41.7G
CHOLESTEROL 6MG   SODIUM 339MG

Three-Greens Salad with Garbanzos

Mixed Melon Salad (recipe on page 38)

REFRESHING FRUIT SALADS

The texture and flavor of fruit make it a perfect ingredient for salads to accompany almost any meal. Serve a fruit salad such as Strawberry and Stilton Salad (page 36) for a tasty appetizer course. For a delicious side dish, try Two-Apple Salad (page 35) or Melon Salad with Peppercorn-Fruit Dressing (page 40). Four-Berry Salad (page 36) and Autumn Fruit Salad (page 45) are sweet salads that you can serve as desserts.

Be creative with these recipes—if the specific fruit used in the recipe isn't available, substitute one that is in season. You can also mix and match the salad dressings, such as Burgundy-Poppy Seed Dressing (page 38), with your own combinations of fresh or canned fruit.

CARROT-PINEAPPLE CONGEALED SALADS

1 (8-ounce) can crushed pineapple in juice, undrained
1¾ cups unsweetened orange juice
2 envelopes unflavored gelatin
2 tablespoons sugar
2 cups shredded carrot
Vegetable cooking spray
Green leaf lettuce (optional)
¼ cup plus 2 tablespoons pineapple low-fat yogurt

Drain pineapple, reserving juice. Set pineapple aside. Combine reserved pineapple juice and orange juice in a small saucepan. Sprinkle gelatin over juice mixture; let stand 1 minute. Add sugar; cook over low heat, stirring constantly, until gelatin and sugar dissolve. Chill gelatin mixture until consistency of unbeaten egg white.

Gently fold pineapple and carrot into gelatin mixture. Spoon mixture evenly into six ½-cup molds coated with cooking spray. Cover and chill until firm.

Unmold salads onto individual lettuce-lined salad plates, if desired; top each serving with 1 tablespoon yogurt. Yield: 6 servings.

PER SERVING: 108 CALORIES (4% FROM FAT)
FAT 0.5G (SATURATED FAT 0.2G)
PROTEIN 3.6G   CARBOHYDRATE 23.4G
CHOLESTEROL 1MG   SODIUM 21MG

CRANBERRY-WALDORF GELATIN SALAD

Be sure to use regular gelatin in this recipe; sugar-free gelatin won't produce the same results.

2 (3-ounce) packages cranberry-flavored gelatin
1¾ cups boiling water
¾ cup cold water
¾ cup diced Red Delicious apple
¾ cup diced Golden Delicious apple
½ cup seedless green grapes, quartered
¼ cup finely chopped pecans
Vegetable cooking spray
½ (8-ounce) block nonfat cream cheese, softened
¾ cup low-fat sour cream
2 tablespoons sugar
¼ teaspoon vanilla extract
Lettuce leaves
Apple slices (optional)
Chopped pecans (optional)

Combine gelatin and boiling water in a bowl; stir until gelatin dissolves. Stir in cold water. Cover and chill 1½ hours or until consistency of unbeaten egg white. Fold in diced apple, grapes, and ¼ cup pecans. Spoon into a 5-cup gelatin mold coated with cooking spray. Chill until firm.

Beat cream cheese at medium speed of an electric mixer until smooth. Add sour cream, sugar, and vanilla; beat well.

Invert mold onto a serving plate; cut salad into 8 pieces. Serve on individual lettuce-lined salad plates; top each salad with 2 tablespoons cream cheese mixture. If desired, garnish with apple slices and chopped pecans. Yield: 8 servings.

PER SERVING: 180 CALORIES (27% FROM FAT)
FAT 5.4G (SATURATED FAT 1.9G)
PROTEIN 4.5G   CARBOHYDRATE 28.9G
CHOLESTEROL 11MG   SODIUM 153MG

TWO-APPLE SALAD

¼ cup finely shredded carrot
¼ cup sliced green onions
1 medium-size Red Delicious apple, quartered
    and cut into julienne strips
1 medium-size Granny Smith apple, quartered
    and cut into julienne strips
1 small fennel bulb, trimmed and cut into
    julienne strips
1 tablespoon water
1 tablespoon white wine vinegar
2 teaspoons vegetable oil
½ teaspoon sugar
¼ teaspoon salt
Fennel fronds, chopped (optional)

Combine first 5 ingredients in a bowl; toss well, and set aside.

Combine water and next 4 ingredients in a small bowl; stir with a wire whisk until blended. Add to apple mixture, tossing gently to coat. Arrange evenly on individual salad plates. Garnish with fennel fronds, if desired. Yield: 4 (1-cup) servings.

Note: The secret of this salad is to slice the apples and fennel into julienne strips—small matchlike pieces.

PER SERVING: 70 CALORIES (33% FROM FAT)
FAT 2.6G (SATURATED FAT 0.4G)
PROTEIN 1.1G   CARBOHYDRATE 11.9G
CHOLESTEROL 0MG   SODIUM 153MG

Two-Apple Salad

Fruit Salad with Vanilla Yogurt and Raspberry Puree

1 (10-ounce) package frozen raspberries in
    light syrup, thawed
2 teaspoons cornstarch
½ teaspoon vanilla extract
1 (8-ounce) carton plain nonfat yogurt
1 (8-ounce) carton vanilla low-fat yogurt
1 cup sliced fresh strawberries
1 cup fresh blueberries
⅓ cup fresh raspberries (about ⅓ half-pint)
8 small clusters seedless green grapes (about
    ½ pound)

Position knife blade in food processor bowl; add raspberries. Process 1 minute or until smooth. Pour puree through a wire-mesh strainer into a saucepan, discarding seeds; add cornstarch to pan, stirring well. Bring mixture to a boil over medium-high heat, stirring constantly. Cook, stirring constantly, 1 minute. Remove from heat; stir in vanilla. Set aside, and cool.

Combine yogurts; stir well. Spoon onto several layers of paper towels; spread evenly to ½-inch thickness. Cover with paper towels; let stand 5 minutes. Spoon into a bowl.

Pour 2 tablespoons raspberry mixture onto one side of each of eight salad plates, forming an even pool. Spoon 2 tablespoons yogurt onto each plate opposite raspberry mixture. Arrange fruit over each serving. Serve immediately. Yield: 8 servings.

Per Serving: 119 Calories (6% from Fat)
Fat 0.8g (Saturated Fat 0.3g)
Protein 3.8g Carbohydrate 25.7g
Cholesterol 2mg Sodium 43mg

Four-Berry Salad

2 cups fresh blackberries
2 cups fresh blueberries
2 cups fresh raspberries
2 cups fresh strawberries
1 (8-ounce) carton vanilla low-fat yogurt
½ cup nonfat sour cream
2 tablespoons cream sherry
2 tablespoons lemon juice
1½ tablespoons honey
3 tablespoons slivered almonds, toasted

Place berries in a large bowl, tossing gently to combine.

Combine yogurt, sour cream, sherry, lemon juice, and honey in a small bowl; stir well.

Spoon berry mixture evenly into individual serving bowls. Top evenly with yogurt mixture and almonds. Yield: 8 servings.

Per Serving: 137 Calories (17% from Fat)
Fat 2.6g (Saturated Fat 0.4g)
Protein 4.1g Carbohydrate 25.5g
Cholesterol 1mg Sodium 33mg

Strawberry and Stilton Salad

2 cups sliced fresh strawberries
2 tablespoons chopped fresh basil
2 tablespoons raspberry vinegar
½ teaspoon sugar
1 teaspoon olive oil
1 teaspoon water
4 cups gourmet salad greens
¼ cup crumbled Stilton cheese or feta
    cheese
4 (1-ounce) slices French bread

Combine strawberries, basil, raspberry vinegar, and sugar in a bowl; toss well to coat. Cover and chill mixture 1 hour.

Strain mixture through a wire-mesh strainer into a jar, reserving liquid. Set strawberries aside. Add oil and water to jar. Cover tightly, and shake vigorously.

Arrange salad greens evenly on individual salad plates. Top each serving with ½ cup strawberries, 2 teaspoons dressing, and 1 tablespoon cheese. Serve with French bread. Yield: 4 servings.

PER SERVING: 158 CALORIES (23% FROM FAT)
FAT 4.0G (SATURATED FAT 1.5G)
PROTEIN 5.3G   CARBOHYDRATE 26.1G
CHOLESTEROL 7MG   SODIUM 275MG

FESTIVE CRANBERRY-PEAR SALAD

1¼ cups fresh cranberries
⅓ cup sugar
⅓ cup water
2 cups cubed fresh pear
½ cup diced celery
2 tablespoons minced walnuts
¼ teaspoon ground nutmeg
Dash of ground allspice
Lettuce leaves (optional)

Combine first 3 ingredients in a small saucepan; bring to a boil. Cook over medium-high heat 6 minutes or until cranberries pop, stirring often. Remove from heat, and cool completely.

Combine cranberry mixture, pear, and next 4 ingredients in a bowl; stir gently. Serve on lettuce leaves, if desired. Yield: 6 (½-cup) servings.

PER SERVING: 99 CALORIES (15% FROM FAT)
FAT 1.6G (SATURATED FAT 0.1G)
PROTEIN 0.9G   CARBOHYDRATE 22.0G
CHOLESTEROL 0MG   SODIUM 11MG

CITRUS SALAD WITH HONEY-LIME DRESSING

¼ cup lime juice
1 tablespoon plus 1 teaspoon honey
1 tablespoon plus 1 teaspoon reduced-calorie chili sauce
1 tablespoon water
Dash of freshly ground pepper
2 cups torn Bibb lettuce
2 cups torn iceberg lettuce
2 cups torn curly endive
2 medium-size pink grapefruit, peeled and sectioned
2 large oranges, peeled and sectioned
½ small ripe avocado, peeled and cut into 18 thin slices

Combine first 5 ingredients in a small bowl; stir with a wire whisk until blended. Cover and chill.

Combine lettuces and endive; toss well. Place 1 cup lettuce mixture on each individual salad plate. Arrange grapefruit sections, orange sections, and avocado evenly on lettuce; drizzle lime mixture evenly over salads. Yield: 6 servings.

PER SERVING: 95 CALORIES (27% FROM FAT)
FAT 2.8G (SATURATED FAT 0.4G)
PROTEIN 1.8G   CARBOHYDRATE 18.3G
CHOLESTEROL 0MG   SODIUM 9MG

FYI

To squeeze more juice from a lemon or lime, let the fruit come to room temperature first. If you forget to set it out ahead of time, microwave the whole lemon or lime for about 10 seconds. Once it reaches room temperature, press and roll the fruit on the counter using the palm of your hand. If you're going to need grated rind, be sure to grate the rind before juicing the fruit.

Burgundy-Poppy Seed Dressing

MIXED MELON SALAD
(pictured on page 32)

1 small ripe pineapple (about 2 pounds)
3 cups ripe cantaloupe balls
2 cups watermelon balls
2 cups ripe honeydew melon balls
Burgundy-Poppy Seed Dressing

Peel and core pineapple; cut into 1-inch cubes (about 5 cups). Combine pineapple, cantaloupe, watermelon, and honeydew in a large bowl.

Pour Burgundy-Poppy Seed Dressing over fruit, and toss to coat. Cover and chill before serving. Yield: 8 (1-cup) servings.

BURGUNDY-POPPY SEED DRESSING
¼ cup plus 2 tablespoons sugar
3 tablespoons minced onion
⅛ teaspoon salt
¼ cup plus 2 tablespoons water
⅓ cup Burgundy or other dry red wine
1 teaspoon unflavored gelatin
1½ tablespoons cold water
1½ teaspoons poppy seeds

Combine first 3 ingredients in a saucepan; add ¼ cup plus 2 tablespoons water and wine. Cook over medium heat until sugar dissolves, stirring often.

Sprinkle gelatin over cold water in a small bowl; let stand 1 minute. Add gelatin mixture to wine mixture, stirring until gelatin dissolves. Remove from heat; stir in poppy seeds. Cover and chill thoroughly. Yield: 1 cup.

PER SERVING: 155 CALORIES (6% FROM FAT)
FAT 1.1G (SATURATED FAT 0.3G)
PROTEIN 1.9G   CARBOHYDRATE 37.7G
CHOLESTEROL 0MG   SODIUM 58MG

MELON-BLACKBERRY SALAD

Thin shreds of lemon rind taste less bitter than grated rind. To cut shreds, peel wide rind strips using a vegetable peeler; then cut them into shreds with a knife.

½ cup water
1 teaspoon (1-inch) shreds of lemon rind
3 tablespoons fresh lemon juice
3 tablespoons honey
2½ cups diced honeydew melon
2 cups diced cantaloupe
1½ cups fresh blackberries
Fresh mint sprigs (optional)

Combine first 4 ingredients in a small saucepan; cook over low heat 2 minutes. Remove from heat, and spoon into a bowl; cover and chill.

Combine melons and berries in a large bowl. Pour lemon juice mixture over fruit; toss gently. Garnish with mint sprigs, if desired. Yield: 6 (1-cup) servings.

PER SERVING: 96 CALORIES (4% FROM FAT)
FAT 0.4G (SATURATED FAT 0.1G)
PROTEIN 1.1G   CARBOHYDRATE 25.0G
CHOLESTEROL 0MG   SODIUM 13MG

Cantaloupe-Blueberry Salad

CANTALOUPE-BLUEBERRY SALAD

1½ cups orange low-fat yogurt
1 tablespoon lemon juice
1½ teaspoons poppy seeds
1 teaspoon grated orange rind
1 medium cantaloupe (about 3 pounds)
12 Boston lettuce leaves
2 cups fresh blueberries

Combine first 4 ingredients, stirring well. Cover and chill.

Peel and seed cantaloupe; cut lengthwise into 32 slices.

Arrange cantaloupe slices evenly on individual lettuce-lined serving plates. Top each serving with ¼ cup blueberries and 3 tablespoons yogurt mixture. Yield: 8 servings.

PER SERVING: 108 CALORIES (8% FROM FAT)
FAT 1.0G (SATURATED FAT 0.2G)
PROTEIN 2.8G CARBOHYDRATE 24.0G
CHOLESTEROL 0MG   SODIUM 39MG

MELON SALAD WITH PEPPERCORN-FRUIT DRESSING

¾ cup fresh or frozen sliced peaches, thawed
½ cup sliced fresh strawberries
1 tablespoon minced fresh mint
1 teaspoon sugar
½ teaspoon green peppercorns
1½ teaspoons olive oil
½ teaspoon red wine vinegar
21 (¼-inch-thick) slices honeydew (about 1 small)
14 (¼-inch-thick) slices cantaloupe (about 1 small)
Fresh mint sprigs (optional)

Combine first 7 ingredients in container of an electric blender or food processor; cover and process until smooth. Pour mixture through a wire-mesh strainer into a bowl; press mixture with back of a spoon against sides of strainer to squeeze out liquid. Discard solids remaining in stainer. Cover and chill dressing thoroughly.

Arrange melon slices evenly on individual salad plates; drizzle evenly with dressing. Garnish with mint sprigs, if desired. Yield: 7 servings.

PER SERVING: 81 CALORIES (14% FROM FAT)
FAT 1.3G (SATURATED FAT 0.3G)
PROTEIN 1.2G CARBOHYDRATE 18.4G
CHOLESTEROL 0MG SODIUM 16MG

ICY-HOT WATERMELON SALAD

2 cups seeded watermelon balls
2 tablespoons diced jicama
2 tablespoons canned chopped green chiles
2 tablespoons balsamic vinegar
1 teaspoon vegetable oil
¼ teaspoon dried crushed red pepper
⅛ teaspoon garlic powder
Green leaf lettuce (optional)

Combine first 3 ingredients in a large bowl, and toss gently.

Combine vinegar and next 3 ingredients; stir well. Pour over watermelon mixture; toss gently. Cover and chill 4 hours.

Line individual salad plates with leaf lettuce, if desired. Spoon watermelon mixture onto plates, using a slotted spoon. Yield: 2 (1-cup) servings.

PER SERVING: 90 CALORIES (31% FROM FAT)
FAT 3.1G (SATURATED FAT 0.8G)
PROTEIN 1.5G CARBOHYDRATE 16.0G
CHOLESTEROL 0MG SODIUM 32MG

PEACH-RASPBERRY SALAD

1 (10-ounce) package frozen raspberries in light syrup, thawed
1 tablespoon raspberry vinegar
8 medium-size ripe peaches
3 tablespoons lemon juice
Curly leaf lettuce (optional)
¼ cup sliced almonds, toasted
½ cup fresh raspberries (optional)

Place raspberries in container of an electric blender or food processor; cover and process until smooth. Press puree through a wire-mesh strainer into a bowl, discarding seeds. Add vinegar to puree; stir well, and set aside.

Cut peaches in half lengthwise; remove pits. Slice halves lengthwise into ¼-inch-thick slices, leaving slices attached ½ inch from stem end. Brush peaches with lemon juice.

Arrange leaf lettuce on individual salad plates, if desired. Arrange peaches evenly over lettuce, letting slices fan out slightly.

Drizzle each salad with 2 tablespoons raspberry mixture, and sprinkle evenly with toasted almonds. Garnish with fresh raspberries, if desired. Serve immediately. Yield: 8 servings.

PER SERVING: 118 CALORIES (15% FROM FAT)
FAT 2.0G (SATURATED FAT 0.2G)
PROTEIN 2.1G CARBOHYDRATE 25.8G
CHOLESTEROL 0MG SODIUM 1MG

Peach-Raspberry Salad

Pear and Arugula Salad

PEAR AND ARUGULA SALAD

2 cups water
2 tablespoons lemon juice
2 medium-size fresh pears
¼ cup plain nonfat yogurt
3 tablespoons reduced-calorie mayonnaise
1 tablespoon white wine vinegar
2 teaspoons sugar
¼ teaspoon ground white pepper
1 bunch fresh arugula
Fresh blueberries (optional)

Combine water and lemon juice in a bowl, stirring well.

Peel and core pears; quarter lengthwise. Slice quarters lengthwise into ¼-inch-thick slices, leaving slices attached ½ inch from stem end. Dip pear slices in lemon juice mixture, and drain well. Set aside.

Combine yogurt and next 4 ingredients in a small bowl; stir well with a wire whisk.

Remove stems from arugula, and arrange leaves evenly on individual salad plates. Arrange pears over arugula, letting slices fan out slightly. Drizzle each salad with 2 tablespoons yogurt mixture. Garnish with fresh blueberries, if desired. Serve immediately. Yield: 4 servings.

PER SERVING: 111 CALORIES (28% FROM FAT)
FAT 3.5G (SATURATED FAT 0.0G)
PROTEIN 1.5G CARBOHYDRATE 20.4G
CHOLESTEROL 4MG SODIUM 97MG

PEPPERED PEARS WITH JARLSBERG CHEESE

3 medium-size ripe pears
Vegetable cooking spray
1 teaspoon reduced-calorie margarine
6 Boston lettuce leaves
2 tablespoons lemon juice
½ teaspoon sugar
½ teaspoon Dijon mustard
1 tablespoon chopped fresh chives
¼ cup (1 ounce) shredded reduced-fat
    Jarlsberg cheese
Dash of freshly ground pepper
Fresh chives (optional)

Peel and core pears; cut in half lengthwise, and set aside.

Coat a large nonstick skillet with cooking spray; add margarine. Place over medium heat; cook until margarine melts. Add pears; sauté 10 to 15 minutes or until pears are tender, turning often. Transfer hot pears to lettuce-lined salad plates; set aside.

Add lemon juice, sugar, and mustard to skillet; cook over medium heat until bubbly. Drizzle lemon juice mixture over pears. Sprinkle with chopped chives, cheese, and pepper. Garnish with fresh chives, if desired. Yield: 6 servings.

PER SERVING: 75 CALORIES (25% FROM FAT)
FAT 2.1G (SATURATED FAT 0.9G)
PROTEIN 1.7G   CARBOHYDRATE 13.6G
CHOLESTEROL 4MG   SODIUM 31MG

Peppered Pears with Jarlsberg Cheese

STUFFED PEAR SALAD

½ cup nonfat ricotta cheese
2 tablespoons golden raisins
1 tablespoon honey
⅛ teaspoon ground nutmeg
2 firm ripe red pears
½ teaspoon lemon juice
2 cups torn watercress
Piquant Dressing
1½ tablespoons pine nuts, toasted

Combine first 4 ingredients in a small bowl, stirring well. Set aside.

Core pears; cut each in half lengthwise. Brush cut sides of pears with lemon juice.

Place watercress on individual salad plates, and top with pear halves. Spoon cheese mixture evenly onto pear halves. Drizzle Piquant Dressing over pears, and sprinkle with pine nuts. Serve immediately. Yield: 4 servings.

PIQUANT DRESSING

¼ cup unsweetened applesauce
1 tablespoon white balsamic vinegar
1 teaspoon sugar
⅛ teaspoon salt
⅛ teaspoon pepper

Combine all ingredients in a small bowl, stirring mixture well. Cover and chill. Yield: ¼ cup plus 1 tablespoon.

PER SERVING: 136 CALORIES (19% FROM FAT)
FAT 2.8G (SATURATED FAT 0.4G)
PROTEIN 5.6G   CARBOHYDRATE 26.7G
CHOLESTEROL 3MG   SODIUM 99MG

GREENS WITH PEARS AND WALNUTS

Watercress has small, crisp, dark green leaves with a slightly bitter, peppery taste. If watercress is unavailable, increase the Bibb lettuce to 3 cups.

¼ cup plus 2 tablespoons plain nonfat yogurt
1 tablespoon sherry vinegar
1 tablespoon honey
¼ teaspoon salt
¼ teaspoon ground mace
1 head Belgian endive
2 cups torn Bibb lettuce
1 cup loosely packed watercress leaves
3 Seckel pears, cored and thinly sliced
2½ tablespoons finely chopped walnuts, toasted

Combine first 5 ingredients in a small bowl, stirring well. Cover and chill 1 hour.

Core endive, and separate into spears. Arrange endive, lettuce, and watercress evenly on individual salad plates. Arrange pear slices evenly over greens. Top each serving with 2 tablespoons yogurt mixture; sprinkle with toasted walnuts. Yield: 4 servings.

PER SERVING: 101 CALORIES (29% FROM FAT)
FAT 3.2G (SATURATED FAT 0.2G)
PROTEIN 3.3G   CARBOHYDRATE 16.2G
CHOLESTEROL 0MG   SODIUM 190MG

FRUIT SALAD WITH CURRY DRESSING

2 cups coarsely chopped Red Delicious apple
2 cups coarsely chopped Anjou pear
3 tablespoons lime juice
1 cup fresh orange sections
¾ cup seedless red grape halves
½ cup sliced fresh strawberries
½ cup peeled, sliced kiwifruit
Curry Dressing

Combine first 3 ingredients in a large bowl; toss well. Add orange sections and next 3 ingredients; toss gently. Spoon Curry Dressing over salad; toss gently to coat. Yield: 7 (1-cup) servings.

CURRY DRESSING
⅔ cup plain low-fat yogurt
1 tablespoon honey
1 teaspoon lime juice
¼ teaspoon curry powder

Combine all ingredients in a small bowl; stir well. Yield: ¾ cup.

PER SERVING: 108 CALORIES (8% FROM FAT)
FAT 0.9G (SATURATED FAT 0.3G)
PROTEIN 2.1G CARBOHYDRATE 25.6G
CHOLESTEROL 1MG SODIUM 16MG

Fruit Salad with Curry Dressing

AUTUMN FRUIT SALAD

1 (8-ounce) carton low-fat sour cream
¼ cup firmly packed brown sugar
½ teaspoon ground cinnamon
1¾ cups sliced banana
1½ cups chopped apple
1½ cups chopped pear
1¼ cups fresh orange sections

Combine first 3 ingredients; stir well. Combine fruit in a bowl, and toss well. Spoon fruit onto individual salad plates; top with sour cream mixture. Yield: 7 (1-cup) servings.

PER SERVING: 171 CALORIES (23% FROM FAT)
FAT 4.4G (SATURATED FAT 2.5G)
PROTEIN 2.0G CARBOHYDRATE 34.0G
CHOLESTEROL 12MG SODIUM 16MG

SUMMER FRUIT SALAD IN LEMONADE GLAZE

1 (11-ounce) can mandarin oranges in water, undrained
¼ teaspoon unflavored gelatin
¼ cup frozen lemonade concentrate, thawed and undiluted
1 teaspoon poppy seeds
2 cups fresh cherries, pitted and halved
2 cups sliced fresh peaches
1½ cups sliced fresh plums

Drain oranges, reserving ¼ cup liquid. Combine reserved liquid and gelatin in a small nonaluminum saucepan; let stand 1 minute. Add lemonade concentrate; stir well. Bring to a boil; boil, stirring constantly, 2 minutes. Remove from heat; stir in poppy seeds. Cover and chill 3 hours or until thickened.

Combine oranges, cherries, peaches, and plums; toss gently. Pour lemonade mixture over fruit, and toss gently. Yield: 6 (1-cup) servings.

PER SERVING: 85 CALORIES (10% FROM FAT)
FAT 0.9G (SATURATED FAT 0.2G)
PROTEIN 1.3G CARBOHYDRATE 19.7G
CHOLESTEROL 0MG SODIUM 3MG

Vegetable-Rice Salad in Tomato Cups (recipe on page 51)

GRAIN & PASTA SALADS

*R*ice, barley, and bulgur have served as menu staples in many cultures for thousands of years. But it is unlikely that the first consumers of these grains envisioned salads like the ones featured here. For example, barley is tossed with black beans, corn, and avocado in the Mexican-inspired Barley and Black Bean Salad (page 48). Plain white rice is boldly seasoned and served in tomato shells for Vegetable-Rice Salad in Tomato Cups (page 51).

Pasta-lovers have likewise transformed pasta into salad creations, using various shapes, sizes, and flavors. On pages 58 and 59, you'll find a simple macaroni salad as well as several unusual salads calling for high-flavor herbs and seasonings.

Barley and Black Bean Salad

BARLEY AND BLACK BEAN SALAD

3 cups cooked pearl barley (cooked without
   salt or fat)
2 cups drained canned black beans
1½ cups frozen whole-kernel corn, thawed
1½ cups diced tomato
1 cup frozen English peas, thawed
1 cup peeled, chopped ripe avocado
¼ cup chopped fresh cilantro
½ teaspoon salt
¼ teaspoon pepper
½ cup water
2 tablespoons fresh lemon juice
1 tablespoon freshly grated onion
1 tablespoon vegetable oil
2 cloves garlic, minced
Romaine lettuce leaves
18 (¼-inch-thick) slices peeled ripe avocado
18 (¼-inch-thick) wedges tomato (about
    1 medium tomato)
Lemon wedges (optional)

Combine first 9 ingredients in a large bowl; toss gently. Combine water and next 4 ingredients in a jar; cover tightly, and shake vigorously. Pour over barley mixture; toss gently. Spoon barley mixture evenly onto individual lettuce-lined plates, using a slotted spoon. Top each salad with 2 avocado slices and 2 tomato wedges. Serve warm or at room temperature. Garnish with lemon wedges, if desired. Yield: 9 servings.

Note: For tangier flavor, add a squeeze of fresh lemon juice just before serving.

PER SERVING: 244 CALORIES (26% FROM FAT)
FAT 7.1G (SATURATED FAT 1.2G)
PROTEIN 8.7G   CARBOHYDRATE 40.3G
CHOLESTEROL 0MG   SODIUM 267MG

TABBOULEH-VEGETABLE SALAD

1 cup bulgur (cracked wheat), uncooked
2 cups canned no-salt-added chicken broth
1 clove garlic, minced
1 (15-ounce) can whole baby corn, drained
1¼ cups sliced green onions
½ cup minced fresh mint
½ cup minced fresh parsley
½ cup crumbled feta cheese
¼ cup sliced ripe olives
¼ cup fat-free Italian dressing
3 tablespoons fresh lemon juice
5 sun-dried tomatoes (packed in oil), drained
     and cut into thin strips
2 cloves garlic, minced
1 (14-ounce) can artichoke hearts, drained and
     quartered
Romaine lettuce leaves (optional)
Lemon slices (optional)

Combine first 3 ingredients in a medium sauce-pan; bring to a boil.

Cover, reduce heat, and simmer 15 minutes or until bulgur is tender and liquid is absorbed. Let mixture cool.

Cut each ear of corn into thirds. Combine corn, bulgur, green onions, and next 9 ingredients in a large bowl; toss well. Cover and chill bulgur mixture at least 2 hours.

If desired, spoon bulgur mixture into a lettuce-lined serving bowl, and garnish with lemon slices. Yield: 8 (1-cup) servings.

PER SERVING: 143 CALORIES (19% FROM FAT)
FAT 3.0G (SATURATED FAT 1.4G)
PROTEIN 5.9G   CARBOHYDRATE 25.1G
CHOLESTEROL 6MG   SODIUM 462MG

Tabbouleh-Vegetable Salad

Chilled Red Beans and Rice

CHILLED RED BEANS AND RICE

¼ cup reduced-calorie Italian dressing
3 tablespoons water
2 tablespoons white vinegar
½ teaspoon dried oregano
¼ teaspoon ground red pepper
¼ teaspoon dried thyme
⅛ teaspoon freshly ground black pepper
1 cup cooked long-grain rice (cooked without salt or fat), chilled
1 cup sliced celery
¾ cup chopped onion
¾ cup chopped tomato
1 (15-ounce) can red kidney beans, drained
Celery leaves (optional)

Combine first 7 ingredients in a jar. Cover tightly, and shake vigorously. Chill.

Combine dressing, rice, sliced celery, chopped onion, tomato, and kidney beans in a bowl; toss well. Cover and chill. Garnish with celery leaves, if desired. Yield: 5 (1-cup) servings.

PER SERVING: 138 CALORIES (5% FROM FAT)
FAT 0.7G (SATURATED FAT 0.1G)
PROTEIN 6.4G CARBOHYDRATE 27.5G
CHOLESTEROL 0MG SODIUM 300MG

BLACK-EYED PEA AND RICE SALAD

3 cups water
½ cup chopped onion
½ cup chopped celery
¼ teaspoon salt
¼ teaspoon pepper
4 ounces Canadian bacon, coarsely chopped
2 (15-ounce) cans black-eyed peas, drained
1 (10-ounce) package frozen turnip greens,
     thawed
1½ cups long-grain rice, uncooked
1 tablespoon drained, minced hot peppers in
     vinegar

Combine first 8 ingredients in a large saucepan. Bring to a boil; stir in rice. Cover, reduce heat, and simmer 25 minutes or until rice is tender and liquid is absorbed. Add hot peppers; toss well. Serve warm or chilled. Yield: 8 (1-cup) servings.

PER SERVING: 233 CALORIES (7% FROM FAT)
FAT 1.9G (SATURATED FAT 0.5G)
PROTEIN 11.3G   CARBOHYDRATE 42.7G
CHOLESTEROL 7MG   SODIUM 465MG

VEGETABLE-RICE SALAD IN TOMATO CUPS

(pictured on page 46)

6 large tomatoes
3 cups cooked long-grain rice (cooked without
     salt or fat)
1 (15-ounce) can no-salt-added black beans,
     drained
1 (10-ounce) package frozen whole-kernel
     corn, thawed
½ cup chopped purple onion
½ cup reduced-fat olive oil vinaigrette
1 tablespoon chopped fresh cilantro
Fresh cilantro sprig (optional)

Cut top off each tomato. Scoop out pulp, leaving ¼-inch-thick shells. Chop pulp to measure 1 cup;

reserve remaining pulp for another use. Invert tomato shells on paper towels; let stand 30 minutes.

Combine chopped pulp, rice, and next 5 ingredients. Chill 30 minutes; spoon into tomato shells. Garnish with cilantro, if desired. Yield: 6 servings.

PER SERVING: 290 CALORIES (16% FROM FAT)
FAT 5.3G (SATURATED FAT 0.5G)
PROTEIN 9.0G   CARBOHYDRATE 55.7G
CHOLESTEROL 0MG   SODIUM 179MG

Tomato Cups

Cut a scalloped edge on top of each cup.

Scoop out the pulp to make a shell.

Invert tomato cups on paper towels to drain.

Antipasto Rice Salad

1 cup long-grain rice, uncooked
1 cup frozen artichoke hearts, cooked and
    quartered
1 cup drained canned kidney beans
1 cup sliced fresh mushrooms
¾ cup diced turkey salami
½ cup finely chopped purple onion
½ cup fat-free Italian dressing
1 teaspoon dried oregano
Lettuce leaves (optional)

Cook rice according to package directions, omitting salt and fat. Rinse with cold water; drain.

Combine rice, artichoke, and next 6 ingredients, stirring well. Cover and chill; stir occasionally.

Serve on individual lettuce-lined salad plates, if desired. Yield: 7 (1-cup) servings.

PER SERVING: 179 CALORIES (12% FROM FAT)
FAT 2.4G (SATURATED FAT 0.7G)
PROTEIN 7.3G CARBOHYDRATE 31.8G
CHOLESTEROL 12MG SODIUM 390MG

Rice Primer

Take a trip down the grain aisle of the supermarket to see the wide array of rices now available. Even the most popular white rice comes as short-, medium-, and long-grain; the shorter the grain, the softer and more moist the end product is. Long-grain rice is preferred for most salads and side dishes.

For a robust-flavored dish, select basmati, jasmine, or one of the other aromatic rices. They smell delightful while cooking and add interest to meals. Brown rices have a crunchy texture and nutty flavor.

With so many different types of rice available, it's important to check package directions for specific liquid requirements and cooking times. Avoid overcooking, and don't stir the rice while it cooks (except for risotto).

Curried Jasmine Rice Salad

Jasmine rice has a somewhat soft texture when cooked. If it isn't available, substitute basmati or regular long-grain rice.

2 cups water
1 cup jasmine rice, uncooked
1¼ cups shredded red cabbage
1¼ cups shredded carrot
⅓ cup minced fresh chives
2 tablespoons minced pickled ginger
1 teaspoon curry powder
⅓ cup unsweetened orange juice
1 tablespoon lime juice
1 tablespoon white wine vinegar
2 teaspoons olive oil
1 teaspoon sesame oil
¼ teaspoon salt
¼ teaspoon freshly ground pepper
Red cabbage leaves (optional)
3 tablespoons pine nuts, toasted
3 tablespoons flaked coconut, toasted

Bring water to a boil in a medium saucepan; stir in rice. Cover, reduce heat, and simmer 20 minutes or until rice is tender and liquid is absorbed. Remove from heat; fluff rice with a fork, and cool.

Arrange shredded cabbage and carrot in a steamer basket over boiling water. Cover and steam 5 minutes or until crisp-tender. Transfer vegetables to a large bowl; stir in chives and ginger. Add rice; toss gently. Set aside.

Cook curry powder in a small skillet over medium heat, stirring constantly, 2 minutes or until fragrant. Remove from heat. Add orange juice and next 6 ingredients to curry powder; stir well. Pour curry mixture over rice; toss gently. Cover and let stand 30 minutes, stirring occasionally.

Spoon rice mixture onto individual cabbage leaf-lined salad plates, if desired. Sprinkle evenly with pine nuts and coconut. Yield: 11 (½-cup) servings.

PER SERVING: 116 CALORIES (30% FROM FAT)
FAT 3.9G (SATURATED FAT 1.3G)
PROTEIN 2.0G CARBOHYDRATE 18.8G
CHOLESTEROL 0MG SODIUM 95MG

RICE SALAD WITH ROASTED CHILES

4 whole fresh green chiles (about 10 ounces)
1 medium cucumber
2 cups cooked long-grain rice (cooked without salt or fat)
1 cup chopped sweet red pepper
½ cup frozen whole-kernel corn, thawed
½ teaspoon grated lime rind
2½ teaspoons fresh lime juice
3 tablespoons minced shallot
2 tablespoons chopped fresh cilantro
2 tablespoons red wine vinegar
2 tablespoons olive oil
1 tablespoon water
¼ teaspoon salt
¼ teaspoon freshly ground pepper
¼ teaspoon brown sugar
Fresh cilantro sprigs (optional)
Cucumber slices (optional)

Cut chiles in half lengthwise; remove and discard seeds and membranes. Place chiles, skin side up, on a baking sheet, and flatten with palm of hand. Broil 5½ inches from heat (with electric oven door partially opened) 10 to 15 minutes or until charred. Place chiles in ice water until cool. Remove from water; peel and discard skins.

Chop chiles, and place in a large bowl. Peel cucumber; cut in half lengthwise. Cut each half crosswise into thin slices; add to chopped chile. Add rice and next 4 ingredients; toss well.

Combine shallot and next 7 ingredients in a jar. Cover tightly, and shake vigorously. Pour over rice mixture; toss gently. Cover and chill thoroughly. If desired, garnish with cilantro sprigs and cucumber slices. Yield: 5 (1-cup) servings.

PER SERVING: 125 CALORIES (22% FROM FAT)
FAT 3.0G (SATURATED FAT 0.4G)
PROTEIN 2.6G   CARBOHYDRATE 23.1G
CHOLESTEROL 0MG   SODIUM 124MG

Rice Salad with Roasted Chiles

GARDEN RICE SALAD

1 cup long-grain rice, uncooked
½ cup frozen English peas
½ cup chopped cucumber
½ cup chopped sweet red pepper
½ cup chopped celery
¼ cup chopped green onions
¼ cup chopped fresh parsley
3 tablespoons sliced ripe olives
½ cup nonfat sour cream
2 tablespoons fresh lemon juice
1½ teaspoons dried Italian seasoning
¼ teaspoon salt

Cook rice according to package directions, omitting salt and fat. Rinse with cold water; drain.

Arrange peas in a steamer basket over boiling water. Cover and steam 2 minutes or until tender. Drain. Combine rice, peas, cucumber, and next 5 ingredients; toss gently. Cover and chill.

Combine sour cream, lemon juice, Italian seasoning, and salt in a bowl; stir well. Cover and chill.

Just before serving, combine rice mixture and sour cream mixture; toss gently. Yield: 5 (1-cup) servings.

PER SERVING: 184 CALORIES (6% FROM FAT)
FAT 1.3G (SATURATED FAT 0.3G)
PROTEIN 5.6G CARBOHYDRATE 36.7G
CHOLESTEROL 0MG SODIUM 231MG

WILD RICE AND APRICOT SALAD

1 cup wild rice, uncooked
3 cups water
5 shallots, halved (about ¼ pound)
2 teaspoons olive oil, divided
½ cup thinly sliced green onions
½ cup dried apricots, cut into ¼-inch strips
2 tablespoons chopped fresh parsley
2 tablespoons water
2 tablespoons balsamic vinegar
¼ teaspoon grated orange rind
¼ teaspoon salt
⅛ teaspoon pepper

Combine rice and 3 cups water in a saucepan; bring to a boil. Cover, reduce heat, and simmer 45 minutes. Drain and set aside.

Toss shallot halves with 1 teaspoon oil in a shallow baking dish. Bake at 400° for 20 minutes or until shallot halves are softened and edges are dark brown.

Combine rice, shallot, green onions, apricot, and parsley in a large bowl; toss gently.

Combine remaining 1 teaspoon oil, 2 tablespoons water, and remaining 4 ingredients; stir with a wire whisk. Pour over rice mixture; toss gently. Yield: 4 (1-cup) servings.

PER SERVING: 239 CALORIES (11% FROM FAT)
FAT 2.8G (SATURATED FAT 0.4G)
PROTEIN 7.7G CARBOHYDRATE 49.3G
CHOLESTEROL 0MG SODIUM 158MG

Quick Tip

You can chop parsley and other herbs on a cutting board with a knife, but for easier cleanup and faster results, try this method. Rinse and dry the parsley; then clip the leaves with kitchen scissors over the measuring cup or measuring spoon.

Wild Rice and Apricot Salad

Toss-and-Serve Wild Rice Salad

1 cup canned no-salt-added chicken broth
1 cup quick-cooking wild rice, uncooked
2 cups frozen broccoli flowerets
6 fresh asparagus spears, cut into 1-inch pieces
½ cup seeded, chopped tomato
¼ cup shredded carrot
Fresh Basil Vinaigrette
Fresh basil sprigs (optional)

Combine chicken broth and rice in a saucepan; bring to a boil over medium heat. Reduce heat, and simmer, uncovered, 5 minutes. Drain; set aside.

Arrange broccoli and asparagus in a steamer basket over boiling water. Cover and steam 7 to 9 minutes or just until tender; cool.

Combine rice, steamed vegetables, tomato, and carrot in a large bowl; toss gently. Shake Fresh Basil Vinaigrette vigorously, and pour over salad; toss gently. Garnish with basil sprigs, if desired. Yield: 4 (1-cup) servings.

Fresh Basil Vinaigrette
2 tablespoons crumbled feta cheese
1 tablespoon minced fresh basil
2 tablespoons white wine vinegar
2 tablespoons olive oil
2 teaspoons lemon juice
¼ teaspoon salt
⅛ teaspoon pepper

Combine all ingredients in a jar; cover tightly, and shake vigorously. Chill. Yield: ⅓ cup.

PER SERVING: 240 CALORIES (32% FROM FAT)
FAT 8.6G (SATURATED FAT 1.5G)
PROTEIN 8.4G CARBOHYDRATE 34.1G
CHOLESTEROL 3MG SODIUM 233MG

Couscous Salad with Creamy Roasted Garlic Dressing

Although there are several varieties of parsley, flat-leaf (sometimes called Italian) parsley is one of the most strongly flavored.

1 large head garlic
1½ cups canned low-sodium chicken broth
1 cup couscous, uncooked
2 tablespoons nonfat mayonnaise
2 tablespoons red wine vinegar
¼ teaspoon salt
¼ teaspoon freshly ground pepper
¾ cup chopped sweet red pepper
½ cup chopped fresh flat-leaf parsley
¼ cup finely chopped celery

Peel outer skin from garlic head. Cut off top one-third of head. Place garlic, cut side up, in center of a piece of heavy-duty aluminum foil. Fold foil over garlic, sealing tightly. Bake at 350° for 1 hour or until garlic is soft. Remove from oven; cool 10 minutes. Remove and discard papery skin from garlic. Squeeze pulp from each clove; set pulp aside.

Bring broth to a boil in a saucepan. Remove from heat. Add couscous; cover and let stand 5 minutes or until couscous is tender and liquid is absorbed. Fluff couscous with a fork.

Combine mayonnaise and next 3 ingredients in a small bowl; stir well. Add garlic pulp; stir well.

Combine couscous, red pepper, parsley, and celery in a large bowl; add mayonnaise mixture, and toss well. Cover and chill 3 hours. Yield: 4 (1-cup) servings.

Note: To save time, substitute commercial roasted garlic for fresh roasted garlic.

PER SERVING: 104 CALORIES (9% FROM FAT)
FAT 1.0G (SATURATED FAT 0.1G)
PROTEIN 4.4G CARBOHYDRATE 20.7G
CHOLESTEROL 0MG SODIUM 296MG

Cold Couscous and Cucumber Salad

COLD COUSCOUS AND CUCUMBER SALAD

¼ cup sugar
¼ cup white wine vinegar
¼ teaspoon salt
1 cup seeded, diced cucumber
1 cup water
1 cup couscous, uncooked
1 teaspoon dried dillweed
40 Belgian endive leaves (about 4 heads)
16 (¼-inch-thick) slices tomato
Yogurt Dressing
Fresh dillweed sprigs (optional)

Combine first 3 ingredients in a small bowl; stir well. Add cucumber; toss well. Cover and chill.

Bring water to a boil in a saucepan; remove from heat. Add couscous; cover and let stand 5 minutes or until couscous is tender and liquid is absorbed. Fluff with a fork. Combine couscous, cucumber mixture, and dried dillweed. Cover and chill.

Place 5 endive leaves and 2 slices tomato on each individual salad plate. Spoon chilled couscous mixture evenly over tomato and endive. Drizzle 2 tablespoons Yogurt Dressing over each salad. Garnish with fresh dillweed sprigs, if desired. Serve immediately. Yield: 8 servings.

YOGURT DRESSING
½ cup plain nonfat yogurt
½ cup nonfat sour cream
¼ teaspoon dried dillweed
⅛ teaspoon salt

Combine all ingredients in a small bowl, stirring well. Yield: 1 cup.

PER SERVING: 142 CALORIES (1% FROM FAT)
FAT 0.2G (SATURATED FAT 0.1G)
PROTEIN 5.5G CARBOHYDRATE 29.3G
CHOLESTEROL 0MG SODIUM 138MG

Cool Couscous Salad

1 cup plus 2 tablespoons no-salt-added chicken
   broth
¾ cup couscous, uncooked
2 cups seeded, chopped tomato
1 cup chopped sweet red pepper
½ cup chopped celery
½ cup seeded, chopped cucumber
¼ cup chopped green onions
¼ cup chopped fresh parsley
3 tablespoons balsamic vinegar
1 tablespoon olive oil
1 tablespoon Dijon mustard
½ teaspoon grated lemon rind
¼ teaspoon black pepper

Bring broth to a boil in a saucepan; stir in couscous. Remove from heat; cover and let stand 5 minutes or until couscous is tender and liquid is absorbed; fluff with a fork. Uncover and cool 10 minutes.

Combine couscous, tomato, and next 5 ingredients in a large bowl, and toss gently.

Combine vinegar and remaining 4 ingredients in a small bowl; stir with a wire whisk.

Add vinegar mixture to couscous mixture; toss to coat. Serve chilled or at room temperature. Yield: 6 (1-cup) servings.

PER SERVING: 121 CALORIES (23% FROM FAT)
FAT 3.1G (SATURATED FAT 0.4G)
PROTEIN 3.7G   CARBOHYDRATE 19.8G
CHOLESTEROL 0MG   SODIUM 117MG

Creamy Macaroni Salad

⅔ cup low-fat sour cream
⅓ cup light mayonnaise
2 tablespoons chopped fresh parsley
2 tablespoons sweet pickle relish
1 tablespoon spicy brown mustard
¼ teaspoon ground white pepper
4 cups cooked elbow macaroni (about 8
   ounces uncooked pasta), cooked without
   salt or fat
1 cup sliced green onions
1 cup frozen English peas, thawed
¾ cup (3 ounces) diced reduced-fat sharp
   Cheddar cheese
½ cup diced carrot
½ cup diced green pepper
½ cup sliced celery
½ cup diced cooked lean ham (about 2
   ounces)

Combine first 6 ingredients in a large bowl, and stir well. Add macaroni and remaining ingredients; toss well to coat. Cover and chill. Yield: 8 (1-cup) servings.

PER SERVING: 229 CALORIES (29% FROM FAT)
FAT 7.5G (SATURATED FAT 0.7G)
PROTEIN 9.9G   CARBOHYDRATE 28.8G
CHOLESTEROL 15MG   SODIUM 203MG

Creamy Macaroni Salad

SANTA BARBARA PASTA SALAD

1 (16-ounce) package frozen baby lima beans
3 cups cooked orecchiette (about 1¾ cups
    uncooked small bowl-shaped pasta),
    cooked without salt or fat
1½ cups diced sweet red pepper
1 cup finely chopped onion
1 cup peeled, chopped tomatillos (about 4
    large)
1 cup fresh corn kernels (about 3 ears)
⅓ cup minced fresh cilantro
2 tablespoons white wine vinegar
2 tablespoons extra-virgin olive oil
¾ teaspoon salt
1 (4.5-ounce) can chopped green chiles,
    undrained

Cook beans in boiling water to cover 18 minutes or until tender. Drain well.

Combine beans, pasta, and remaining ingredients in a large bowl. Serve at room temperature or chilled. Yield: 10 (1-cup) servings.

PER SERVING: 159 CALORIES (20% FROM FAT)
FAT 3.6G (SATURATED FAT 0.5G)
PROTEIN 6.2G CARBOHYDRATE 27.0G
CHOLESTEROL 0MG SODIUM 248MG

PASTA PRIMAVERA SALAD

3 tablespoons white wine vinegar
1 teaspoon olive oil
¼ teaspoon dried basil
⅛ teaspoon salt
Dash of garlic powder
Dash of freshly ground pepper
3 ounces fresh asparagus (about 3 spears)
4 ounces spaghetti, uncooked
½ cup frozen English peas, thawed
¼ cup julienne-sliced sweet red pepper
1 tablespoon freshly grated Parmesan cheese
2 cherry tomatoes, quartered

Combine first 6 ingredients in a small bowl, stirring well. Set aside.

Snap off tough ends of asparagus. Remove scales with a knife or vegetable peeler, if desired. Cut asparagus into 1-inch pieces. Arrange asparagus in a steamer basket over boiling water. Cover; steam 4 minutes or until crisp-tender. Rinse with cold water.

Break spaghetti in half; cook according to package directions, omitting salt and fat. Rinse with cold water, and drain. Place spaghetti in a bowl. Add vinegar mixture, asparagus, peas, and red pepper; toss well. Sprinkle with cheese, and top with cherry tomatoes. Cover and chill thoroughly. Yield: 4 servings.

PER SERVING: 150 CALORIES (13% FROM FAT)
FAT 2.2G (SATURATED FAT 0.5G)
PROTEIN 6.0G CARBOHYDRATE 26.2G
CHOLESTEROL 1MG SODIUM 130MG

GARDEN PASTA SALAD

3 cups cooked rotini (corkscrew pasta),
    cooked without salt or fat
1 cup broccoli flowerets
1 cup quartered cherry tomatoes
¾ cup diced cooked lean ham (3 ounces)
½ cup sliced carrot
½ cup vertically sliced purple onion
⅓ cup sliced ripe olives
¼ cup grated Parmesan cheese
2 tablespoons chopped fresh basil or
    2 teaspoons dried basil
2 tablespoons chopped fresh parsley or
    2 teaspoons dried parsley
¼ cup nonfat sour cream
¼ cup low-fat buttermilk
¼ cup light Ranch-style dressing

Combine first 10 ingredients in a large bowl. Combine sour cream, buttermilk, and dressing; stir well. Pour over salad, and toss to coat. Yield: 7 (1-cup) servings.

PER SERVING: 174 CALORIES (29% FROM FAT)
FAT 5.6G (SATURATED FAT 1.2G)
PROTEIN 8.2G CARBOHYDRATE 22.5G
CHOLESTEROL 9MG SODIUM 362MG

Spinach Salad with Asiago Cheese and Croutons (recipe on page 64)

SALADS FROM THE GARDEN

With fresh produce available almost year-round, the possibilities are limitless for creating fresh vegetable salads. Packaged gourmet salad greens are perfect for the wilted greens salad on page 63. And you can prepare the Roasted Red Pepper and Asparagus Salad (page 74) any season of the year using fresh peppers and asparagus.

Take advantage of this wide variety to introduce new salad greens and other vegetables into your family's meals. The following recipes feature unusual combinations of vegetables and dressings as well as low-fat versions of basic recipes, including Seven-Layer Italian Salad (page 67), Three-Bean Salad with Balsamic Dressing (page 70), Apple-Cabbage Slaw (page 71), and Old-Fashioned Potato Salad (page 75).

Wilted Greens with Warm Bacon Dressing

WILTED GREENS WITH WARM BACON DRESSING

2 cups water
½ cup shelled English peas
6 cups gourmet salad greens (about ¼ pound)
½ cup thinly sliced green onions
4 slices turkey bacon, diced
¼ cup water
2 tablespoons red wine vinegar
2 tablespoons fresh lemon juice
Coarsely ground pepper (optional)

Bring 2 cups water to a boil in a saucepan; add peas. Cover and cook 7 minutes or until crisp-tender. Drain and rinse under cold running water; drain well.

Combine peas, salad greens, and onions in a bowl.

Cook bacon in a nonstick skillet over medium heat 4 minutes or until crisp. Add ¼ cup water, vinegar, and lemon juice; cook 2 minutes. Immediately pour over salad; toss gently to coat. Sprinkle with pepper, if desired. Yield: 4 (1½-cup) servings.

PER SERVING: 56 CALORIES (42% FROM FAT)
FAT 2.6G (SATURATED FAT 0.7G)
PROTEIN 4.0G   CARBOHYDRATE 5.1G
CHOLESTEROL 10MG   SODIUM 195MG

Quick Tip

To remove the papery skin from garlic, press a clove with the flat side of a knife blade; the clove will slip out from the skin. Next, cut the peeled clove into fine pieces. Or to save time, use minced garlic from a jar.

BABY GREENS WITH TOASTED SESAME CROUTONS

If you can't find mixed baby salad greens, use 4 cups of your favorite salad greens instead.

12 (¼-inch-thick) slices French baguette
1½ teaspoons olive oil
1 tablespoon sesame seeds, toasted
Vegetable cooking spray
1 medium carrot, scraped
4 cups mixed baby salad greens
⅓ cup nonfat mayonnaise
¼ cup plain nonfat yogurt
1 tablespoon grated Parmesan cheese
1 tablespoon fat-free milk
1 teaspoon cider vinegar
¼ teaspoon salt
¼ teaspoon freshly ground pepper
1 clove garlic, minced

Brush both sides of bread slices with oil; sprinkle 1 side of slices with sesame seeds. Place slices, seed side up, on a baking sheet coated with cooking spray. Bake at 400° for 10 minutes or until crisp and golden; cool.

Slice carrot lengthwise into very thin slices to form ribbons, using a vegetable peeler and applying firm pressure. Reserve center core of carrot for another use. Combine carrot strips and salad greens in a large bowl, tossing gently.

Combine mayonnaise and remaining 7 ingredients, stirring until smooth; pour over salad greens mixture. Toss gently. Place salad evenly on individual salad plates. Top each serving with 2 sesame croutons, seed side up. Yield: 6 (1-cup) servings.

PER SERVING: 107 CALORIES (29% FROM FAT)
FAT 3.4G (SATURATED FAT 0.6G)
PROTEIN 3.7G   CARBOHYDRATE 15.6G
CHOLESTEROL 2MG   SODIUM 411MG

SPINACH SALAD WITH ASIAGO CHEESE AND CROUTONS

(pictured on page 60)

Use a vegetable peeler or a cheese plane to shave thin slices of cheese.

6 (¾-ounce) slices French bread, cut into
    ¾-inch cubes
1 teaspoon dried oregano
1 clove garlic, crushed
6 cups loosely packed torn fresh spinach
3 cups loosely packed torn radicchio
⅓ cup balsamic vinegar
1½ tablespoons water
1 teaspoon sugar
¼ teaspoon pepper
2 cloves garlic, minced
2 teaspoons extra-virgin olive oil
1½ ounces shaved Asiago cheese

Combine first 3 ingredients in a large zip-top plastic bag. Seal bag; shake to coat bread cubes. Turn bread cube mixture out onto a 15- x 10- x 1-inch jellyroll pan; arrange bread cubes in a single layer. Bake at 350° for 15 minutes or until toasted. Set croutons aside.

Combine spinach and radicchio in a large bowl; toss gently.

Combine vinegar and next 4 ingredients in a small saucepan; bring to a boil. Reduce heat, and simmer, uncovered, 2 minutes. Remove from heat; add oil, stirring constantly with a wire whisk. Immediately pour vinegar mixture over salad; toss well. Spoon onto serving platter; top with croutons and cheese. Serve immediately. Yield: 6 (1½-cup) servings.

PER SERVING: 128 CALORIES (29% FROM FAT)
FAT 4.1G (SATURATED FAT 1.5G)
PROTEIN 6.6G CARBOHYDRATE 16.8G
CHOLESTEROL 5MG SODIUM 288MG

WILTED SPINACH-CHEESE SALAD

1 (10-ounce) bag fresh spinach
1 cup sliced fresh strawberries
2 ounces reduced-fat Cheddar cheese, cut into
    ½-inch cubes
Sweet-Hot Dressing

Combine first 3 ingredients in a large bowl. Pour Sweet-Hot Dressing over salad, and toss gently. Place salad evenly on individual salad plates. Serve immediately. Yield: 6 servings.

SWEET-HOT DRESSING
2 teaspoons cornstarch
¼ cup water
⅔ cup unsweetened apple juice
⅓ cup cider vinegar
1 tablespoon brown sugar
1 teaspoon poppy seeds
1 teaspoon Dijon mustard

Combine cornstarch and water in a small non-aluminum saucepan, stirring until smooth. Stir in apple juice and remaining ingredients. Bring to a boil; boil, stirring constantly, 1 minute. Serve immediately. Yield: 1⅓ cups.

PER SERVING: 74 CALORIES (28% FROM FAT)
FAT 2.3G (SATURATED FAT 1.1G)
PROTEIN 4.4G CARBOHYDRATE 10.1G
CHOLESTEROL 6MG SODIUM 134MG

Greek Salad with Feta and Olives

GREEK SALAD WITH FETA AND OLIVES

8 cups torn romaine lettuce
4 cups torn escarole
1½ cups thinly sliced purple onion, separated
   into rings
1½ cups thinly sliced green pepper rings
1½ cups thinly sliced sweet red pepper rings
½ cup thinly sliced radishes
¼ cup pitted, sliced kalamata olives
2 tomatoes, each cut into 8 wedges
Oregano Vinaigrette
⅓ cup crumbled feta cheese

Combine first 8 ingredients in a large bowl.
Pour Oregano Vinaigrette over salad, and toss well.
Sprinkle feta cheese over salad. Yield: 10 (1⅔-cup)
servings.

OREGANO VINAIGRETTE
¼ cup dry white wine
¼ cup fresh lemon juice
1 tablespoon extra-virgin olive oil
1 tablespoon chopped fresh oregano or
   1 teaspoon dried oregano
¼ teaspoon salt
¼ teaspoon pepper
4 cloves garlic, minced

Combine all ingredients in a jar; cover tightly,
and shake vigorously. Yield: about ⅔ cup.

PER SERVING: 67 CALORIES (43% FROM FAT)
FAT 3.2G (SATURATED FAT 1.0G)
PROTEIN 2.5G CARBOHYDRATE 7.7G
CHOLESTEROL 4MG SODIUM 155MG

Seven-Layer Italian Salad

SEVEN-LAYER ITALIAN SALAD

A tangy dressing that contains very little fat enhances crisp fresh vegetables in this salad.

3 cups shredded iceberg lettuce
1 medium-size sweet red pepper, cut into strips
1 medium cucumber, sliced
2 cups yellow or red teardrop tomatoes, halved
1 medium-size sweet yellow pepper, cut into
   ½-inch pieces
1 cup thinly sliced celery
¾ cup sliced green onions
¼ cup red wine vinegar
¼ cup water
1 tablespoon vegetable oil
2 teaspoons Dijon mustard
1 teaspoon dried Italian seasoning
1 teaspoon minced fresh garlic
½ teaspoon pepper
¼ teaspoon hot sauce
½ cup (2 ounces) shredded nonfat mozzarella
   cheese
Sweet red pepper rings (optional)

Layer first 7 ingredients in a 3-quart bowl.
Combine vinegar and next 7 ingredients, stirring with a wire whisk. Pour vinegar mixture over salad. Sprinkle with cheese. Cover and chill. Garnish with red pepper rings, if desired. To serve, place salad evenly on individual salad plates. Yield: 8 servings.

PER SERVING: 61 CALORIES (34% FROM FAT)
FAT 2.3G (SATURATED FAT 0.4G)
PROTEIN 3.8G CARBOHYDRATE 7.6G
CHOLESTEROL 1MG SODIUM 115MG

MARINATED BLACK BEAN SALAD

You can use leftover jicama as a low-fat snack. Cut it into thin strips. To serve, squeeze a lime wedge over the strips, and sprinkle with chili powder.

½ pound dried black beans
1 cup chopped tomato
¾ cup diced sweet red pepper
¾ cup diced zucchini
¾ cup peeled, diced jicama
½ cup sliced green onions
¼ cup diced avocado
1 tablespoon chopped fresh chives
1 teaspoon seeded, minced jalapeño pepper
½ teaspoon cumin seeds, toasted
¼ cup water
1 tablespoon fat-free Italian salad dressing mix
3 tablespoons fresh lime juice
3 tablespoons balsamic vinegar
1 teaspoon olive oil

Sort and wash beans; place in a Dutch oven. Cover with water to a depth of 3 inches above beans. Bring to a boil; boil 5 minutes. Remove from heat. Cover and let stand 1 hour. Drain. Return beans to pan. Cover with water to a depth of 3 inches above beans. Bring to a boil; cover, reduce heat, and simmer 1 hour. Rinse under cold running water; drain well.
Combine beans, tomato, and next 8 ingredients in a large bowl; toss gently.
Combine water and remaining 4 ingredients, stirring well with a wire whisk. Pour over bean mixture; toss gently. Cover; marinate in refrigerator at least 8 hours. Yield: 11 (½-cup) servings.

PER SERVING: 100 CALORIES (13% FROM FAT)
FAT 1.4G (SATURATED FAT 0.2G)
PROTEIN 5.1G CARBOHYDRATE 17.7G
CHOLESTEROL 0MG SODIUM 190MG

WHITE BEAN AND TOMATO SALAD

2 (15-ounce) cans cannellini beans or Great
    Northern beans, drained
1½ cups chopped tomato
⅓ cup shredded fresh basil
¼ cup crumbled feta cheese
¼ cup white balsamic vinegar
1½ tablespoons olive oil
½ teaspoon sugar
¼ teaspoon salt
¼ teaspoon freshly ground pepper
Green leaf lettuce leaves (optional)

Combine first 4 ingredients in a large bowl; set aside.

Combine vinegar and next 4 ingredients in a small jar. Cover tightly, and shake vigorously. Pour vinegar mixture over bean mixture. Let stand at room temperature 30 minutes, stirring occasionally. Serve on individual lettuce-lined salad plates, if desired. Yield: 6 (¾-cup) servings.

PER SERVING: 133 CALORIES (33% FROM FAT)
FAT 4.9G (SATURATED FAT 1.2G)
PROTEIN 5.6G   CARBOHYDRATE 16.3G
CHOLESTEROL 4MG   SODIUM 539MG

Why Balsamic?

Balsamic vinegar, made from the reduced juice of sweet grapes, is sweeter and more full-flavored than other vinegars. Like wine, it is aged in wooden barrels for several years to develop the flavor. And as with any fine, aged wine, it can be expensive.

If you want the rich, mellow flavor of balsamic vinegar without the traditional dark color, use the light-colored version. It has all of the flavor and looks better on white pasta and rice and light-colored vegetables. Find balsamic vinegar on the vinegar aisle in most supermarkets.

GREEN BEAN-POTATO SALAD WITH CITRUS VINAIGRETTE

¾ pound green beans
3 cups cubed red potato (about 1 pound)
½ cup thinly sliced shallot
¼ cup white wine vinegar
1 tablespoon minced fresh basil
1 teaspoon grated orange rind
2 tablespoons fresh orange juice
1 teaspoon grated lemon rind
2 tablespoons fresh lemon juice
1 tablespoon extra-virgin olive oil
¾ teaspoon salt
¼ teaspoon pepper
24 cherry tomatoes, halved (about ¾ pound)
3 cups trimmed watercress (about 1 bunch)

Trim ends from green beans, and remove strings. Arrange beans in a steamer basket over boiling water; cover and steam 8 minutes or until crisp-tender. Place beans in a bowl; set aside.

Arrange potato in steamer basket over boiling water; cover and steam 8 minutes or until crisp-tender. Place potato in a bowl; set aside.

Combine shallot and next 9 ingredients; stir well. Pour ¼ cup shallot mixture over beans, and toss well; cover and chill. Pour ¼ cup shallot mixture over potato, and toss well; cover and chill. Pour remaining shallot mixture over tomato halves, and toss well; cover and chill.

Arrange beans, potato, tomatoes, and watercress evenly on individual salad plates. Drizzle with any remaining shallot mixture. Yield: 6 servings.

PER SERVING: 120 CALORIES (20% FROM FAT)
FAT 2.6G (SATURATED FAT 0.4G)
PROTEIN 3.8G   CARBOHYDRATE 22.4G
CHOLESTEROL 0MG   SODIUM 316MG

Green Bean-Potato Salad with Citrus Vinaigrette

Three-Bean Salad with Balsamic Dressing

THREE-BEAN SALAD WITH BALSAMIC DRESSING

2½ cups (2-inch) sliced green beans (about ½ pound)
⅓ cup balsamic vinegar
¼ cup chopped fresh parsley or 1 tablespoon plus 1 teaspoon dried parsley flakes
¼ cup chopped fresh basil or 1 tablespoon plus 1 teaspoon dried basil
2 tablespoons grated Parmesan cheese
1 tablespoon chopped fresh dillweed or 1 teaspoon dried dillweed
1 tablespoon olive oil
½ teaspoon garlic powder
¼ teaspoon salt
¼ teaspoon pepper
1½ cups sliced carrot
½ cup vertically sliced purple onion
1 (15½-ounce) can garbanzo beans (chick-peas), drained
1 (15-ounce) can kidney beans, drained
1 (14-ounce) can artichoke hearts, drained and coarsely chopped
1 large tomato, cut into 16 wedges
Fresh dillweed sprigs (optional)

Arrange green beans in a steamer basket over boiling water. Cover and steam 2 minutes. Rinse under cold running water; drain well.

Combine vinegar and next 8 ingredients in a large bowl; stir well. Add green beans, carrot, onion, garbanzo beans, kidney beans, and artichoke hearts; toss gently to coat. Serve with tomato wedges; garnish with dillweed sprigs, if desired. Yield: 8 (1-cup) servings.

PER SERVING: 162 CALORIES (18% FROM FAT)
FAT 3.3G (SATURATED FAT 0.6G)
PROTEIN 8.6G   CARBOHYDRATE 27.1G
CHOLESTEROL 1MG   SODIUM 269MG

BEET AND ONION SALAD

6 medium-size fresh beets (about 2¾ pounds)
Vegetable cooking spray
1½ teaspoons olive oil, divided
1 cup (½-inch) vertically sliced onion
3 tablespoons lemon juice
1 teaspoon balsamic vinegar
1 teaspoon Dijon mustard
¼ teaspoon salt
⅛ teaspoon pepper

Leave root and 1 inch of stem on beets; scrub well with a vegetable brush. Place in a Dutch oven; add water to cover. Bring to a boil; cover, reduce heat, and simmer 35 minutes or until beets are tender. Drain. Rinse beets under cold running water. Drain and cool.

Trim off beet stems and roots; rub off skins. Slice beets; set aside. Coat a small skillet with cooking spray; add 1 teaspoon oil, and place over medium heat until hot. Add onion; sauté 6 minutes or until tender. Combine beets and onion in a large bowl; set aside.

Combine remaining ½ teaspoon oil, lemon juice, vinegar, mustard, salt, and pepper; stir well. Pour over vegetables, tossing gently. Yield: 4 (1-cup) servings.

PER SERVING: 97 CALORIES (28% FROM FAT)
FAT 3.0G (SATURATED FAT 0.3G)
PROTEIN 2.5G   CARBOHYDRATE 17.6G
CHOLESTEROL 0MG   SODIUM 287MG

FRUITED BROCCOLI SALAD

3 cups fresh broccoli flowerets
⅓ cup golden raisins
¼ cup sweet onion slices, separated into
    rings
¼ cup light mayonnaise
¼ cup nonfat sour cream
2 tablespoons minced water chestnuts
1 tablespoon white wine vinegar
¼ teaspoon grated orange rind
1 tablespoon fresh orange juice
2 teaspoons sugar
Orange rind strips (optional)

Combine first 3 ingredients in a large bowl, and toss gently.

Combine mayonnaise and next 6 ingredients in a small bowl; stir well. Add mayonnaise mixture to broccoli mixture, and toss gently to coat vegetables. Cover and chill thoroughly. Garnish with orange rind strips before serving, if desired. Yield: 8 (½-cup) servings.

PER SERVING: 56 CALORIES (34% FROM FAT)
FAT 2.1G (SATURATED FAT 0.3G)
PROTEIN 1.6G   CARBOHYDRATE 8.5G
CHOLESTEROL 2MG   SODIUM 66MG

APPLE-CABBAGE SLAW

4 cups very thinly sliced cabbage
2 cups diced Fuji or Red Delicious
    apple (about 1 pound)
½ cup chopped green onions
¼ cup chopped fresh flat-leaf parsley
½ cup low-fat sour cream
¼ cup plain nonfat yogurt
2 tablespoons brown sugar
2 tablespoons cider vinegar
¼ teaspoon salt
⅛ teaspoon pepper
8 thin slices Fuji or Red Delicious
    apple
¼ cup lemon juice

Combine first 4 ingredients in a large bowl; toss well. Combine sour cream and next 5 ingredients; add to cabbage mixture, stirring to coat. Spoon slaw evenly onto individual salad plates.

Combine apple slices and lemon juice. Drain apple; discard juice. Arrange 2 apple slices around each salad. Yield: 4 (1-cup) servings.

PER SERVING: 144 CALORIES (25% FROM FAT)
FAT 4.0G (SATURATED FAT 2.3G)
PROTEIN 3.1G   CARBOHYDRATE 26.8G
CHOLESTEROL 12MG   SODIUM 189MG

MINTED CARROT SALAD

3 cups (¼-inch) diagonally sliced carrot
¼ cup sherry vinegar
3 tablespoons fresh lemon juice
2 teaspoons olive oil
¼ teaspoon salt
¼ teaspoon pepper
1 clove garlic, minced
2 tablespoons raisins
2 tablespoons chopped onion
2 tablespoons chopped fresh parsley
1 tablespoon pine nuts, toasted
1 tablespoon chopped fresh mint

Drop carrot into a large saucepan of boiling water, and return to a boil. Rinse under cold running water; drain well.

Combine vinegar and next 5 ingredients in a large bowl; stir with a wire whisk until blended. Add carrot, raisins, and next 3 ingredients; toss gently. Cover and chill. Stir in mint before serving. Yield: 7 (½-cup) servings.

PER SERVING: 64 CALORIES (38% FROM FAT)
FAT 2.7G (SATURATED FAT 0.4G)
PROTEIN 0.9G   CARBOHYDRATE 8.7G
CHOLESTEROL 0MG   SODIUM 153MG

MARINATED HEARTS OF PALM SALAD

1 pound fresh asparagus spears
4 medium-size plum tomatoes, quartered
    lengthwise
1 (14-ounce) can hearts of palm, drained and
    sliced
½ cup fat-free balsamic vinaigrette
6 Boston lettuce leaves
¼ cup freshly grated Parmesan cheese
½ teaspoon freshly ground pepper

Snap off tough ends of asparagus. Remove scales with a knife or vegetable peeler, if desired. Arrange asparagus in a steamer basket over boiling water. Cover and steam 7 minutes or until crisp-tender. Drain well.

Place asparagus, tomato, and hearts of palm in a shallow dish; add vinaigrette. Cover and marinate in refrigerator 30 minutes.

Drain vegetables, discarding vinaigrette. Arrange vegetables evenly on lettuce-lined salad plates. Sprinkle evenly with cheese and pepper. Yield: 6 servings.

PER SERVING: 70 CALORIES (13% FROM FAT)
FAT 1.0G (SATURATED FAT 0.4G)
PROTEIN 3.9G   CARBOHYDRATE 13.2G
CHOLESTEROL 1MG   SODIUM 479MG

TRIPLE-MUSHROOM SALAD WITH WALNUTS

Olive oil-flavored vegetable cooking spray
1½ cups thinly sliced button mushrooms
1 cup sliced portobello mushroom caps
1 cup thinly sliced shiitake mushroom caps
2 tablespoons chopped fresh parsley
1 tablespoon minced shallot
3 cloves garlic, minced
¼ cup sherry vinegar
1 tablespoon low-sodium soy sauce
2 teaspoons honey
8 cups gourmet salad greens
2 tablespoons chopped walnuts, toasted

Place a large nonstick skillet coated with cooking spray over medium-high heat until hot. Add button mushrooms and next 5 ingredients; sauté 3 minutes or until mushrooms are tender.

Combine vinegar, soy sauce, and honey; add to skillet. Remove from heat. Arrange salad greens evenly on individual salad plates; spoon ⅓ cup mushroom mixture over each serving. Sprinkle each serving with 1½ teaspoons walnuts. Yield: 4 servings.

PER SERVING: 89 CALORIES (29% FROM FAT)
FAT 2.9G (SATURATED FAT 0.2G)
PROTEIN 3.9G   CARBOHYDRATE 11.1G
CHOLESTEROL 0MG   SODIUM 196MG

Preparing Fresh Asparagus

The best fresh asparagus is available in early spring when the sweet, thin stalks are in season. Choose firm, bright green spears with tightly closed tips.

To prepare the fresh spears, snap off the tough stalk of each asparagus spear (about 1 to 2 inches). Remove the scales, if you wish, by scraping each spear with a vegetable peeler or knife.

Marinated Black-Eyed Pea Salad

MARINATED BLACK-EYED PEA SALAD

Vegetable cooking spray
1 cup chopped onion
3 cups shelled black-eyed peas (about 1 pound
    unshelled)
2¼ cups water
¼ cup chopped cooked ham
¼ teaspoon pepper
1 (10½-ounce) can low-sodium chicken broth
2 tablespoons white wine vinegar
1 tablespoon olive oil
1 tablespoon lemon juice
1 teaspoon honey
½ teaspoon salt
½ teaspoon dried dillweed
½ teaspoon dried thyme
¼ teaspoon pepper
2 cloves garlic, crushed
1 cup halved cherry tomatoes
⅓ cup sliced green onions
Spinach leaves (optional)

Coat a large saucepan with cooking spray, and place over medium heat until hot. Add onion; sauté 5 minutes or until tender.

Stir in peas and next 4 ingredients; bring to a boil. Cover, reduce heat, and simmer 30 minutes or until peas are tender, stirring occasionally. Drain and set aside.

Combine vinegar and next 8 ingredients in a large bowl; stir well with a wire whisk.

Add pea mixture, tomato halves, and green onions to vinegar mixture; toss gently. Cover salad, and marinate in refrigerator 8 hours. Spoon into a spinach-lined bowl, if desired. Yield: 8 (1-cup) servings.

PER SERVING: 124 CALORIES (27% FROM FAT)
FAT 3.7G (SATURATED FAT 0.8G)
PROTEIN 7.4G   CARBOHYDRATE 16.8G
CHOLESTEROL 4MG   SODIUM 256MG

Roasting Peppers

Place peppers, skin side up, on a foil-lined baking sheet; flatten with palm of hand.

Broil 3 inches from heat for 12 minutes or until blackened. Place in a zip-top plastic bag; seal and let stand 15 minutes.

Peel and discard the blackened skins. The roasted pepper will be soft and slippery.

ROASTED RED PEPPER AND ASPARAGUS SALAD

2 medium-size sweet red peppers (about ½ pound)
1½ pounds fresh asparagus spears
3 tablespoons red wine vinegar
1 tablespoon water
1 teaspoon dark sesame oil
½ teaspoon freshly ground pepper
¼ teaspoon sugar
⅛ teaspoon salt
8 Bibb lettuce leaves

Cut peppers in half lengthwise; remove and discard seeds and membranes. Place peppers, skin side up, on an aluminum foil-lined baking sheet; flatten with palm of hand. Broil 3 inches from heat (with electric oven door partially opened) 12 minutes or until blackened. Place peppers in a zip-top plastic bag; seal and let stand 15 minutes. Peel and discard skins. Cut peppers into ¼-inch-wide strips. Cover and chill.

Snap off tough ends of asparagus. Remove scales with a knife or vegetable peeler, if desired. Arrange asparagus in a steamer basket over boiling water. Cover and steam 4 minutes or until crisp-tender. Rinse with cold water. Cover and chill.

Combine vinegar and next 5 ingredients in a jar. Cover tightly, and shake vigorously. Chill mixture thoroughly.

Arrange asparagus evenly on individual lettuce-lined salad plates. Arrange pepper strips evenly over asparagus, and drizzle with vinegar mixture. Serve immediately. Yield: 8 servings.

PER SERVING: 28 CALORIES (26% FROM FAT)
FAT 0.8G (SATURATED FAT 0.1G)
PROTEIN 1.7G   CARBOHYDRATE 4.8G
CHOLESTEROL 0MG   SODIUM 39MG

OLD-FASHIONED POTATO SALAD

9 cups cubed round red potato (about 3 pounds)
½ cup diced onion
½ cup diced celery
¼ cup sweet pickle relish or dill pickle relish, drained
3 hard-cooked eggs, chopped
1 clove garlic, minced
¾ cup low-fat sour cream
⅓ cup nonfat mayonnaise
2 tablespoons chopped fresh parsley
1 teaspoon dry mustard
¾ teaspoon salt
¼ teaspoon pepper

Place potato in a Dutch oven; cover with water, and bring to a boil. Cook 8 minutes or until tender. Drain; place in a large bowl. Add onion and next 4 ingredients; toss gently.

Combine sour cream and remaining 5 ingredients; stir well. Pour over potato mixture; toss gently to coat. Cover and chill. Yield: 9 (1-cup) servings.

PER SERVING: 192 CALORIES (21% FROM FAT)
FAT 4.4G (SATURATED FAT 2.1G)
PROTEIN 6.1G   CARBOHYDRATE 32.8G
CHOLESTEROL 78MG   SODIUM 383MG

Old-Fashioned Potato Salad

Pesto Potato Salad

PESTO POTATO SALAD

*The easiest way to cut up dried tomatoes
is to use your kitchen shears.*

½ cup sun-dried tomatoes (packed
   without oil)
½ cup hot water
2 pounds small round red potatoes
Olive oil-flavored vegetable cooking spray
½ cup sliced green onions
2 cloves garlic, minced
⅓ cup reduced-fat Caesar dressing
½ cup nonfat sour cream
2 tablespoons pesto
¼ teaspoon freshly ground pepper

   Coarsely chop tomatoes. Combine tomato and
hot water in a small bowl; let stand 10 minutes.
Drain and set aside.

   Cut potatoes into 1-inch pieces. Cook potato in
boiling water to cover 15 to 17 minutes or until
tender. Drain and cool slightly.

   Coat a large nonstick skillet with cooking spray;
place over medium-high heat until hot. Add
tomato, potato, green onions, and garlic to skillet;
sauté 5 minutes. Add dressing, deglazing skillet by
scraping particles that cling to bottom. Cook 1
minute.

   Combine sour cream, pesto, and pepper in a large
bowl, stirring well. Add potato mixture; toss lightly
until combined. Yield: 6 (1-cup) servings.

PER SERVING: 201 CALORIES (26% FROM FAT)
FAT 5.7G (SATURATED FAT 0.8G)
PROTEIN 6.1G CARBOHYDRATE 32.0G
CHOLESTEROL 3MG SODIUM 446MG

HERB-MARINATED TOMATOES

2 large tomatoes, cut into ½-inch slices
2 tablespoons chopped fresh basil
1 tablespoon chopped fresh parsley
1 tablespoon chopped fresh oregano
1 tablespoon fresh lemon juice
1 teaspoon balsamic vinegar
¼ teaspoon salt
¼ teaspoon freshly ground pepper
Fresh basil sprigs (optional)

   Arrange tomato slices on a platter. Sprinkle with
chopped basil, parsley, and oregano.

   Combine lemon juice and vinegar; drizzle over
tomato. Cover and chill 2 hours. Sprinkle with salt
and pepper. Garnish with basil sprigs, if desired.
Yield: 4 servings.

PER SERVING: 39 CALORIES (16% FROM FAT)
FAT 0.7G (SATURATED FAT 0.1G)
PROTEIN 1.6G CARBOHYDRATE 8.8G
CHOLESTEROL 0MG SODIUM 162MG

Herb-Marinated Tomatoes

Sautéed Citrus (recipe on page 85)

FRUIT ON THE SIDE

Great taste is just one of the many virtues of fruit side dishes. Most recipes require few ingredients and are easy to prepare. For example, Caribbean Bananas (page 83) calls for only bananas, margarine, and three spices. In less than five minutes, you'll have a flavorful dish to serve with chicken or pork.

Raspberry Applesauce (page 82) and Honeyed Pears (page 86) demonstrate the versatility of fruit side dishes— they fit into almost any menu, whether for breakfast, lunch, or dinner. As with many other fruit dishes, you can make them ahead and refrigerate them; then reheat or serve cold.

It's also easy to make substitutions when preparing fruit side dishes. You can often substitute frozen or canned fruit when fresh is unavailable; just thaw, drain, and pat the fruit dry with paper towels before using.

Cinnamon-Crusted Baked Apples

CINNAMON-CRUSTED BAKED APPLES

Butter-flavored vegetable cooking spray
⅓ cup water
5 medium cooking apples
⅓ cup firmly packed brown sugar
¼ cup all-purpose flour
½ teaspoon ground cinnamon
¼ teaspoon ground nutmeg
2 tablespoons reduced-calorie margarine,
    softened

Coat an 11- x 7- x 1½-inch baking dish with cooking spray; pour water into dish. Peel, core, and slice apples. Arrange apple in prepared dish; coat apple lightly with cooking spray.

Combine brown sugar, flour, cinnamon, and nutmeg; cut in margarine with a pastry blender until mixture resembles coarse meal. Sprinkle mixture evenly over apple. Bake, uncovered, at 350° for 30 minutes or until apple is tender. Yield: 8 servings.

PER SERVING: 127 CALORIES (16% FROM FAT)
FAT 2.3G (SATURATED FAT 0.3G)
PROTEIN 0.5G CARBOHYDRATE 28.4G
CHOLESTEROL 0MG SODIUM 30MG

SWEET APPLE AND CHESTNUT SAUTÉ

1 tablespoon margarine
1½ cups diced onion
¾ cup thinly sliced celery
1 cup cooked, shelled, and coarsely chopped chestnuts (about 1 pound in shells)
1 large Granny Smith apple, peeled, cored, and cut into 16 wedges
¼ cup maple syrup
Fresh thyme sprigs (optional)

Melt margarine in a large nonstick skillet over medium heat. Add onion and celery; sauté 4 minutes. Add chestnuts and apple; sauté 8 minutes. Add syrup, and sauté 1 minute. Garnish with thyme sprigs, if desired. Yield: 4 (¾-cup) servings.

PER SERVING: 220 CALORIES (16% FROM FAT)
FAT 3.9G (SATURATED FAT 0.8G)
PROTEIN 2.1G CARBOHYDRATE 45.6G
CHOLESTEROL 0MG SODIUM 57MG

Sweet Apple and Chestnut Sauté

BRANDIED APPLES

½ cup water
2 tablespoons sugar
2 tablespoons raisins
2 tablespoons brandy
½ teaspoon ground cinnamon
4 large Red Delicious apples, cored and sliced

Combine first 5 ingredients in a large saucepan. Bring to a boil over medium heat, stirring until sugar dissolves. Stir in apple. Cover, reduce heat, and simmer 10 minutes or until apple is tender. Yield: 6 (¾-cup) servings.

PER SERVING: 103 CALORIES (4% FROM FAT)
FAT 0.5G (SATURATED FAT 0.1G)
PROTEIN 0.4G CARBOHYDRATE 26.8G
CHOLESTEROL 0MG SODIUM 1MG

WHIPPED APPLE AND RUTABAGA

2 large Rome apples, peeled, cored, and quartered
1 small rutabaga (about 1½ pounds), peeled and thinly sliced
½ cup unsweetened apple juice
2 tablespoons frozen orange juice concentrate, thawed and undiluted
1 tablespoon honey
⅛ teaspoon salt
Dash of ground nutmeg

Place apple and rutabaga in a saucepan; add water to pan to a depth of 1 inch. Bring to a boil; cover, reduce heat, and simmer 1 hour or until tender. Drain. Position knife blade in food processor bowl; add apple mixture, apple juice, and remaining ingredients. Process until smooth. Serve warm or at room temperature. Yield: 8 (½-cup) servings.
Note: Serve this side dish with ham or chicken.

PER SERVING: 81 CALORIES (4% FROM FAT)
FAT 0.4G (SATURATED FAT 0.1G)
PROTEIN 1.2G CARBOHYDRATE 19.7G
CHOLESTEROL 0MG SODIUM 53MG

Raspberry Applesauce

RASPBERRY APPLESAUCE

1 (24-ounce) jar cinnamon-flavored applesauce
2 tablespoons light brown sugar
¾ cup frozen unsweetened raspberries
Fresh raspberries (optional)
Fresh mint sprigs (optional)
Cinnamon sticks (optional)

Combine applesauce and sugar in a saucepan; cook over medium-high heat until hot and bubbly, stirring often. Remove from heat; stir in frozen raspberries. Let stand 5 minutes. Serve applesauce warm or chilled. If desired, garnish with fresh raspberries, mint, and cinnamon sticks. Yield: 6 (½-cup) servings.

Note: Serve with roasted turkey and other side dishes like baked sweet potatoes and English peas.

PER SERVING: 105 CALORIES (3% FROM FAT)
FAT 0.3G (SATURATED FAT 0.0G)
PROTEIN 0.3G CARBOHYDRATE 27.1G
CHOLESTEROL 0MG SODIUM 5MG

PEAR APPLESAUCE WITH AMARETTO

3½ cups peeled, cubed Granny Smith apple
2½ cups peeled, cubed Bartlett pear
2 tablespoons water
2 tablespoons brown sugar
1 tablespoon amaretto

Combine first 3 ingredients in a large saucepan; cover and cook over low heat 40 minutes or until very tender. Mash to desired consistency; stir in sugar and amaretto. Serve at room temperature or chilled. Yield: 4 (¾-cup) servings.

PER SERVING: 143 CALORIES (4% FROM FAT)
FAT 0.7G (SATURATED FAT 0.1G)
PROTEIN 0.5G CARBOHYDRATE 34.8G
CHOLESTEROL 0MG SODIUM 2MG

CARIBBEAN BANANAS

2 medium-size, firm, ripe bananas (about ¾ pound)
1 tablespoon reduced-calorie margarine
½ teaspoon curry powder
⅛ teaspoon ground ginger
⅛ teaspoon chili powder

Cut bananas in half crosswise; then cut in half lengthwise.
Melt margarine in a large nonstick skillet over medium-high heat. Add curry powder, ginger, and chili powder; cook 30 seconds. Add banana; cook 1 minute. Turn banana; cook 1 additional minute. Yield: 2 servings.
Note: This fruit dish is a good accompaniment to poultry entrées.

PER SERVING: 184 CALORIES (18% FROM FAT)
FAT 3.7G (SATURATED FAT 0.8G)
PROTEIN 1.8G CARBOHYDRATE 40.3G
CHOLESTEROL 0MG SODIUM 73MG

HONEYED BANANAS

Serve this sweet side dish with pork or chicken. Or turn it into a dessert by topping it with a scoop of low-fat vanilla ice cream.

6 medium bananas
2 tablespoons lemon juice
½ teaspoon ground cinnamon
2 tablespoons reduced-calorie margarine
3 tablespoons honey

Brush bananas with lemon juice, and sprinkle with cinnamon.
Melt margarine in a large nonstick skillet over medium heat; stir in honey. Add bananas; cook 3 to 4 minutes or until thoroughly heated, turning once. Serve immediately. Yield: 6 servings.

PER SERVING: 152 CALORIES (17% FROM FAT)
FAT 2.9G (SATURATED FAT 0.5G)
PROTEIN 1.1G CARBOHYDRATE 34.2G
CHOLESTEROL 0MG SODIUM 38MG

SPICED CRANBERRIES

1 (12-ounce) bag fresh cranberries
1 cup sugar
1 cup water
¼ teaspoon ground cinnamon
⅛ teaspoon ground ginger
Dash of ground nutmeg

Combine all ingredients in a medium saucepan; bring to a boil over medium-high heat. Reduce heat, and simmer, uncovered, 10 minutes or until cranberries pop, stirring occasionally. Spoon into a bowl; cover and chill. Yield: 10 (¼-cup) servings.

PER SERVING: 94 CALORIES (1% FROM FAT)
FAT 0.1G (SATURATED FAT 0.0G)
PROTEIN 0.1G CARBOHYDRATE 24.4G
CHOLESTEROL 0MG SODIUM 1MG

VERY CHERRY CRANBERRIES

Serve this instead of traditional cranberry sauce with turkey or ham.

1 (12-ounce) package fresh or frozen
   cranberries
1 cup frozen pitted sweet cherries
⅓ cup sugar
½ cup cranberry-cherry drink
1 vanilla bean, split
¼ cup chopped pecans or almonds, toasted

Combine first 5 ingredients in a saucepan, stirring well. Bring to a boil; reduce heat, and simmer, uncovered, 20 minutes or until thickened. Remove and discard vanilla bean. Spoon cranberry mixture into a serving bowl; sprinkle with nuts. Serve warm. Yield: 6 (⅓-cup) servings.

PER SERVING: 134 CALORIES (22% FROM FAT)
FAT 3.3G (SATURATED FAT 1.6G)
PROTEIN 1.1G CARBOHYDRATE 27.0G
CHOLESTEROL 0MG SODIUM 1MG

BROILED GRAPEFRUIT SUPREME

2 large pink grapefruit
2 tablespoons low-sugar orange marmalade
2 teaspoons cream sherry
1 tablespoon brown sugar

Cut grapefruit in half crosswise; remove seeds, and loosen sections. Place grapefruit, cut side up, on rack of a broiler pan. Combine marmalade and sherry. Drizzle over grapefruit; sprinkle with sugar. Broil 5½ inches from heat (with electric oven door partially opened) 6 minutes or until thoroughly heated and sugar melts. Yield: 4 servings.

PER SERVING: 70 CALORIES (3% FROM FAT)
FAT 0.2G (SATURATED FAT 0.0G)
PROTEIN 1.2G CARBOHYDRATE 17.8G
CHOLESTEROL 0MG SODIUM 2MG

HONEYED MANGOES

3 tablespoons dark rum
2 tablespoons honey
½ teaspoon grated lime rind
1 tablespoon fresh lime juice
⅛ teaspoon ground cinnamon
5 cups peeled, sliced ripe mango (about 3
   pounds)

Combine first 5 ingredients in a nonstick skillet; cook over medium-high heat 1 minute, stirring occasionally.

Add mango, and cook 3 minutes, stirring occasionally. Spoon mango mixture evenly into individual serving bowls; spoon remaining rum mixture evenly over mango. Serve warm. Yield: 6 (¾-cup) servings.

Note: See page 26 for tips on slicing mangoes.

PER SERVING: 112 CALORIES (3% FROM FAT)
FAT 0.4G (SATURATED FAT 0.1G)
PROTEIN 0.7G CARBOHYDRATE 29.5G
CHOLESTEROL 0MG SODIUM 3MG

Honeyed Mangoes

SAUTÉED CITRUS

(pictured on page 78)

2 medium-size pink grapefruit
2 large oranges
Vegetable cooking spray
1 tablespoon reduced-calorie margarine
¼ cup cinnamon schnapps
¼ teaspoon orange zest
¼ teaspoon grapefruit zest
Fresh mint sprigs (optional)

Peel and section grapefruit and oranges. Coat a nonstick skillet with cooking spray; add margarine. Place over medium heat until margarine melts. Add schnapps; cook 1 minute. Stir in fruit; cook 2 to 3 minutes. Transfer to a serving dish. Sprinkle with orange zest and grapefruit zest. Garnish with mint, if desired. Yield: 8 (½-cup) servings.

PER SERVING: 64 CALORIES (15% FROM FAT)
FAT 1.1G (SATURATED FAT 0.1G)
PROTEIN 0.8G   CARBOHYDRATE 14.0G
CHOLESTEROL 0MG   SODIUM 14MG

SPICED PEACHES AND PINEAPPLE

3½ tablespoons brown sugar
2 teaspoons cornstarch
⅛ teaspoon whole cloves
⅛ teaspoon ground cloves
1 (8-ounce) can pineapple tidbits in juice,
    undrained
3 cups frozen sliced peaches, thawed

Combine first 4 ingredients in a small saucepan. Stir in pineapple. Cook over medium heat, stirring constantly, until sugar dissolves; stir in peaches.
Bring mixture to a boil; reduce heat, and simmer, uncovered, 5 minutes or until thickened. Remove and discard whole cloves. Yield: 4 (½-cup) servings.

PER SERVING: 126 CALORIES (1% FROM FAT)
FAT 0.1G (SATURATED FAT 0.0G)
PROTEIN 0.9G   CARBOHYDRATE 32.5G
CHOLESTEROL 0MG   SODIUM 6MG

Citrus Sense

To obtain zest, remove only the colored part of skin using a citrus zester.

To section, cut off ends of fruit. Stand fruit on end; cut off skin from top to bottom.

Slice between membranes using a sharp paring knife to remove sections.

HONEYED PEARS

2 medium-size ripe pears
2 tablespoons pear nectar
2 tablespoons honey
2 teaspoons vinegar
⅛ teaspoon ground cinnamon
Dash of salt
Ground cinnamon (optional)

Core pears; cut crosswise into ½-inch slices, and set aside.

Combine nectar and next 4 ingredients in a large nonstick skillet; bring to a boil.

Add pear to honey mixture; reduce heat, and simmer 10 minutes or until pear is tender, turning once. Garnish with additional cinnamon, if desired. Serve warm. Yield: 4 (½-cup) servings.

PER SERVING: 97 CALORIES (4% FROM FAT)
FAT 0.4G (SATURATED FAT 0.0G)
PROTEIN 0.4G CARBOHYDRATE 25.4G
CHOLESTEROL 0MG SODIUM 37MG

POACHED PEARS WITH BLUE CHEESE AND TOASTED WALNUTS

If you're looking for a side dish that has a touch of sweetness yet doesn't go overboard on the sugar, try this tasty pear dish.

4 firm ripe Bartlett pears
1 cup water
½ cup dry red wine
¼ cup lemon juice
2 ounces crumbled blue cheese
2 tablespoons coarsely chopped walnuts, toasted
Watercress sprigs (optional)
Freshly ground pepper (optional)

Peel and core pears; cut each in half lengthwise. Combine water, wine, and lemon juice in a skillet; bring to a boil. Place pear halves, cut side down, in skillet. Cover, reduce heat, and simmer 20 minutes, turning and basting once with wine mixture.

Remove pear from wine mixture, using a slotted spoon. Place pear halves on a serving platter, and sprinkle evenly with cheese and walnuts. If desired, garnish with watercress sprigs and sprinkle with pepper. Yield: 8 servings.

PER SERVING: 88 CALORIES (36% FROM FAT)
FAT 3.5G (SATURATED FAT 1.4G)
PROTEIN 2.4G CARBOHYDRATE 13.7G
CHOLESTEROL 5MG SODIUM 100MG

TANGY PINEAPPLE PUFF

1 (8-ounce) can crushed pineapple in juice, undrained
½ cup fat-free egg substitute
¼ cup fat-free milk
¼ cup no-sugar-added peach spread
2 tablespoons sugar
2 teaspoons prepared mustard
2 (1¼-ounce) slices French bread, cut into ½-inch cubes
Vegetable cooking spray

Drain pineapple, reserving juice; set pineapple aside. Add enough water to pineapple juice to measure ¾ cup.

Combine juice, egg substitute, and next 4 ingredients. Stir in pineapple and bread cubes. Pour into a 1½-quart baking dish coated with cooking spray. Bake at 350° for 1 hour. Serve immediately. Yield: 6 servings.

PER SERVING: 97 CALORIES (5% FROM FAT)
FAT 0.5G (SATURATED FAT 0.1G)
PROTEIN 3.7G CARBOHYDRATE 19.6G
CHOLESTEROL 1MG SODIUM 126MG

Poached Pears with Blue Cheese and Toasted Walnuts

GRILLED PINEAPPLE

To make this recipe even more quickly, buy a peeled, cored fresh pineapple.

1 medium-size fresh pineapple, peeled and
   cored
¼ cup reduced-sodium teriyaki sauce
2 tablespoons brown sugar
2 teaspoons vegetable oil
Vegetable cooking spray

Cut pineapple crosswise into 8 slices; place in a 13- x 9- x 2-inch baking dish. Combine teriyaki sauce, brown sugar, and oil, stirring well. Pour teriyaki mixture over pineapple, turning pineapple to coat. Let stand at room temperature 45 minutes, turning pineapple once. Remove pineapple from marinade; discard marinade.

Coat grill rack with cooking spray, and place on grill over medium-hot coals (350° to 400°). Place pineapple on rack; grill, covered, 2 minutes on each side or until pineapple is tender. Yield: 8 servings.

PER SERVING: 56 CALORIES (16% FROM FAT)
FAT 1.0G (SATURATED FAT 0.1G)
PROTEIN 0.4G CARBOHYDRATE 12.0G
CHOLESTEROL 0MG SODIUM 81MG

Grilled Pineapple

Pineapple Tips

While fresh pineapple is available throughout the year, its peak growing season is from March to July. If allowed to ripen on the vine, fresh pineapple will be very juicy and have a sweet-tart taste.

When selecting, choose a pineapple with a deep golden-brown color and a slightly sweet smell. A ripe pineapple will be a bit soft to the touch. You should be able to pull the leaves from the top without much effort. Avoid fruit that has dark, mushy spots or a woody-looking or whitish appearance.

1. Cut about 1 inch from each end of the pineapple.

2. Stand the pineapple vertically on the cutting board. Using a sharp knife, slice down about ½ inch into the skin. This should remove the eyes from the pineapple flesh.

3. Keep turning the pineapple with one hand and slicing 1-inch-wide bands down in a straight line until the pineapple is peeled.

4. Cut the fruit into quarters. While holding each pineapple quarter firmly, remove the core.

5. Cut the pineapple wedges in half lengthwise; then cut as needed for the recipe.

DRIED FRUIT COMPOTE

1½ cups unsweetened apple cider or pineapple
   juice
½ cup water
3 whole cloves
1 (3-inch) stick cinnamon
1 (8-ounce) bag dried mixed fruit

Combine first 4 ingredients in a saucepan; bring
to a boil.

Add fruit; cover, reduce heat, and simmer 30
minutes or until fruit is tender, stirring occasionally.
Spoon into a bowl; cover and chill. Remove and
discard cloves and cinnamon stick before serving.
Yield: 4 (½-cup) servings.

PER SERVING: 197 CALORIES (1% FROM FAT)
FAT 0.1G (SATURATED FAT 0.0G)
PROTEIN 1.0G   CARBOHYDRATE 50.6G
CHOLESTEROL 0MG   SODIUM 14MG

WARM CURRIED FRUIT

1 (8-ounce) can pineapple chunks in juice,
   undrained
1 (8¼-ounce) can pear halves in juice, drained
   and cut in half
1 (8¼-ounce) can apricot halves in light syrup,
   drained
1 (8¼-ounce) can sliced peaches in water,
   drained
Butter-flavored vegetable cooking spray
1 tablespoon dried cranberries
1 tablespoon reduced-calorie margarine
3 tablespoons brown sugar
2 tablespoons water
1½ teaspoons curry powder
2 teaspoons cornstarch

Drain pineapple; reserve 3 tablespoons juice.
Discard remaining juice. Place pineapple, pear,
apricot, and peaches on paper towels. Pat dry; place
in an 11- x 7- x 1½-inch baking dish coated with
cooking spray. Sprinkle with cranberries; set aside.

Melt margarine in a small saucepan over medium-
high heat. Add brown sugar, water, and curry powder,
stirring well. Cook over medium heat, stirring until
sugar dissolves.

Combine reserved pineapple juice and cornstarch,
stirring until smooth. Add to margarine mixture.
Bring to a boil over medium heat, stirring constantly; boil 1 minute. Pour margarine mixture over
fruit. Cover and chill 8 hours. Bake, uncovered, at
350° for 45 minutes. Yield: 8 (½-cup) servings.

PER SERVING: 71 CALORIES (14% FROM FAT)
FAT 1.1G (SATURATED FAT 0.0G)
PROTEIN 0.5G   CARBOHYDRATE 15.8G
CHOLESTEROL 0MG   SODIUM 16MG

GRILLED HONEY FRUIT SKEWERS

4 medium-size ripe nectarines
2 medium bananas
32 (1-inch) chunks fresh pineapple
2 tablespoons lemon juice
3 tablespoons reduced-calorie margarine,
   melted
3 tablespoons honey
¾ teaspoon ground cinnamon
Vegetable cooking spray
Fresh mint sprig (optional)

Slice each nectarine into 8 wedges; place in a
bowl. Slice each banana into 8 slices. Add banana
and pineapple to nectarine. Pour lemon juice over
fruit mixture; toss well. Cover; chill at least 1 hour.

Soak 16 (6-inch) wooden skewers in water for 30
minutes. Drain fruit mixture, reserving juice.
Thread fruit alternately onto skewers. Combine
reserved juice, margarine, honey, and cinnamon.

Coat grill rack with cooking spray; place on grill
over medium coals (300° to 350°). Brush kabobs
lightly with honey mixture, and place on rack. Grill,
uncovered, 2 minutes on each side, basting occasionally with remaining honey mixture. Garnish
with a mint sprig, if desired. Yield: 8 servings.

PER SERVING: 127 CALORIES (24% FROM FAT)
FAT 3.4G (SATURATED FAT 0.5G)
PROTEIN 1.0G   CARBOHYDRATE 26.4G
CHOLESTEROL 0MG   SODIUM 42MG

Grilled Honey Fruit Skewers

Orecchiette with Fresh Vegetables and Herbs (recipe on page 107)

GRAIN & PASTA SIDE DISHES

*T*he popularity of pastas and grains is easy to understand. While these foods have been around for centuries, we now know they are rich in complex carbohydrates and contain little, if any, fat. On a less scholarly note, they simply taste good!

This chapter demonstrates how to preserve the low-fat characteristics of pasta, rice, barley, and other grains. The recipes are heavy on fat-free seasonings and light on the typical additions of butter and cream. Fresh cilantro and several ground herbs give brown rice a flavor boost for Mediterranean Rice Pilaf (page 98). And you keep the fat down in Creamy Macaroni and Cheese (page 104) by using low-fat milk and reduced-fat sharp Cheddar cheese.

Portobello Mushrooms

Portobello mushrooms are large, dark brown mushrooms. When they're cooked, they have a rich, meaty flavor and texture. Portobellos are good candidates for stuffing, grilling, roasting, or broiling.

PORTOBELLO MUSHROOM BARLEY

1 small leek (about ¼ pound)
Olive oil-flavored vegetable cooking spray
1 teaspoon olive oil
5 ounces fresh portobello mushrooms, chopped
1 clove garlic, minced
1 cup quick-cooking barley, uncooked
1⅔ cups canned reduced-sodium beef broth
⅓ cup dry white wine
⅛ teaspoon salt
2 tablespoons grated Parmesan cheese

Remove and discard root, tough outer leaves, and top from leek. Finely chop leek.

Coat a large nonstick skillet with cooking spray; add oil. Place over medium heat until hot. Add chopped leek, mushrooms, and garlic; sauté until mushrooms are tender.

Add barley and next 3 ingredients; bring to a boil. Cover, reduce heat, and simmer 16 to 18 minutes or until barley is tender and most of liquid is absorbed. Remove from heat; let stand 5 minutes. Sprinkle with cheese; serve immediately. Yield: 5 (¾-cup) servings.

PER SERVING: 118 CALORIES (15% FROM FAT)
FAT 2.0G (SATURATED FAT 0.6G)
PROTEIN 4.0G CARBOHYDRATE 20.9G
CHOLESTEROL 2MG SODIUM 102MG

BULGUR-VEGETABLE CASSEROLE

2 cups water
¾ teaspoon salt
1 cup bulgur (cracked wheat), uncooked
2 tablespoons lemon juice, divided
1 teaspoon olive oil
Vegetable cooking spray
2 cups finely chopped onion
1½ cups diced zucchini
2 cloves garlic, minced
1½ cups sliced fresh mushrooms
1½ cups seeded, diced plum tomato
½ cup (2 ounces) shredded sharp Cheddar cheese
½ cup low-fat milk
2 eggs, lightly beaten, or ½ cup fat-free egg substitute

Combine water and salt in a saucepan; bring to a boil. Gradually stir in bulgur; cook, uncovered, over medium-low heat 10 minutes or until water is absorbed, stirring occasionally. Stir in 1 tablespoon lemon juice; set aside.

Heat oil in a large nonstick skillet coated with cooking spray over medium heat. Add onion, and sauté 3 minutes. Add zucchini and garlic; sauté 3 minutes. Add mushrooms and tomato; sauté 4 minutes. Remove from heat. Stir in remaining 1 tablespoon lemon juice; set aside.

Add cheese, milk, and eggs to bulgur mixture; stir mixture well. Spread half of bulgur mixture in a 1½-quart baking dish coated with cooking spray. Spread zucchini mixture evenly over bulgur mixture. Spread remaining bulgur mixture evenly over zucchini mixture.

Cover and bake at 325° for 20 minutes. Uncover and bake 10 additional minutes or until thoroughly heated. Yield: 6 (1-cup) servings.

PER SERVING: 203 CALORIES (29% FROM FAT)
FAT 6.6G (SATURATED FAT 2.9G)
PROTEIN 9.9G CARBOHYDRATE 28.7G
CHOLESTEROL 82MG SODIUM 394MG

CHEESE GRITS SOUFFLÉ

¼ cup quick-cooking grits, uncooked
2 egg yolks
⅔ cup evaporated skimmed milk
½ cup (2 ounces) shredded reduced-fat
   Cheddar cheese, divided
¼ teaspoon salt
¼ teaspoon ground white pepper
6 egg whites
Vegetable cooking spray

Cook grits according to package directions, omitting salt and fat. Remove from heat; cool slightly.

Lightly beat egg yolks in a large bowl. Add grits, milk, ¼ cup cheese, salt, and pepper; stir well.

Beat egg whites at high speed of an electric mixer until stiff peaks form. Fold one-third of egg whites into grits mixture; fold in remaining beaten egg whites. Pour into a 2-quart soufflé dish coated with cooking spray. Sprinkle with remaining ¼ cup cheese. Bake at 375° for 25 to 30 minutes or until puffed and golden. Serve immediately. Yield: 8 servings.

PER SERVING: 79 CALORIES (27% FROM FAT)
FAT 2.4G (SATURATED FAT 1.0G)
PROTEIN 6.6G CARBOHYDRATE 8.0G
CHOLESTEROL 58MG SODIUM 178MG

POLENTA WITH SUN-DRIED TOMATOES

1 cup sun-dried tomatoes (packed without oil)
1 cup hot water
Olive oil-flavored vegetable cooking spray
1 teaspoon olive oil
⅓ cup plus 1½ tablespoons finely chopped
   shallot
2 cloves garlic, crushed
2 (14¼-ounce) cans reduced-sodium chicken
   broth
1½ cups water
½ teaspoon salt
½ teaspoon cracked pepper
1⅓ cups instant polenta
½ cup grated Asiago cheese

Combine tomatoes and hot water in a small bowl. Cover and let stand 15 minutes; drain. Coarsely chop tomatoes; set aside.

Coat a large saucepan with cooking spray; add oil. Place over medium-high heat until hot. Add shallot and garlic; sauté until tender.

Add broth and next 3 ingredients; bring to a boil. Add polenta in a slow, steady stream, stirring constantly. Reduce heat to medium; cook, stirring constantly, 3 to 5 minutes or until thickened. Remove from heat. Stir in chopped tomato and cheese. Serve warm. Yield: 11 (½-cup) servings.

PER SERVING: 100 CALORIES (17% FROM FAT)
FAT 1.9G (SATURATED FAT 0.7G)
PROTEIN 3.7G CARBOHYDRATE 16.7G
CHOLESTEROL 3MG SODIUM 279MG

Polenta with Wild Mushroom Sauce

POLENTA WITH WILD MUSHROOM SAUCE

*Don't limit yourself to mushroom sauce—you can
serve other hearty sauces with this polenta.*

1⅓ cups yellow cornmeal
½ teaspoon salt
4 cups water
Vegetable cooking spray
1 tablespoon olive oil
2 cloves garlic, minced
2 sprigs fresh thyme
1 sprig fresh rosemary
6½ cups thinly sliced fresh shiitake mushroom
    caps (about 1 pound mushrooms)
1 cup canned crushed tomatoes
⅓ cup dry white wine
3 tablespoons balsamic vinegar
⅛ teaspoon salt
⅛ teaspoon pepper
2 tablespoons chopped fresh parsley
3 tablespoons freshly grated Parmesan cheese
Fresh thyme sprigs (optional)

Place cornmeal and ½ teaspoon salt in a large
saucepan. Gradually add water, stirring constantly
with a wire whisk. Bring to a boil; reduce heat to
medium. Cook, uncovered, 15 minutes, stirring
often. Spoon polenta into an 8½- x 4½- x 3-inch
loafpan coated with cooking spray, spreading
evenly. Press heavy-duty plastic wrap onto surface
of polenta, and chill 2 hours or until firm.

Heat oil in a large nonstick skillet over medium
heat. Add garlic, 2 thyme sprigs, and rosemary
sprig; cook 3 minutes or just until garlic begins to
brown. Stir in mushrooms and next 5 ingredients;
bring to a boil. Cover, reduce heat, and simmer 15
minutes, stirring occasionally. Remove and discard
thyme and rosemary sprigs. Add parsley; cook,
uncovered, 5 minutes. Remove from heat; set
aside, and keep warm.

Invert polenta onto a cutting board; cut crosswise
into 12 slices. Place slices on a baking sheet coated
with cooking spray. Broil 5½ inches from heat
(with electric oven door partially opened) 5 minutes on each side or until golden.

Place 2 polenta slices on each individual serving
plate. Top each serving with about ⅓ cup mushroom sauce and 1½ teaspoons cheese. Garnish with
thyme sprigs, if desired. Yield: 6 servings.

PER SERVING: 178 CALORIES (21% FROM FAT)
FAT 4.2G (SATURATED FAT 1.0G)
PROTEIN 6.0G CARBOHYDRATE 30.0G
CHOLESTEROL 2MG SODIUM 359MG

COCONUT-PINEAPPLE RICE

*This lively side dish will brighten up a simple
fish or pork entrée.*

2 teaspoons olive oil
1 cup diced onion
2 teaspoons minced fresh thyme or
    ½ teaspoon dried thyme
¼ teaspoon pepper
¾ cup basmati or long-grain rice, uncooked
1½ cups diced fresh pineapple
1 cup water
½ cup chopped green onions
½ cup unsweetened pineapple juice
2 tablespoons flaked sweetened coconut
½ teaspoon salt

Heat oil in a large saucepan over medium heat.
Add diced onion, thyme, and pepper, and sauté
2 minutes.

Add rice; cook 1 minute. Stir in pineapple and
remaining ingredients; bring mixture to a boil.
Cover, reduce heat, and simmer 20 minutes or
until rice is tender and liquid is absorbed. Yield:
4 (1-cup) servings.

PER SERVING: 228 CALORIES (15% FROM FAT)
FAT 3.9G (SATURATED FAT 1.3G)
PROTEIN 3.6G CARBOHYDRATE 45.4G
CHOLESTEROL 0MG SODIUM 306MG

CHILE-RICE CASSEROLE

For variety, use reduced-fat sharp Cheddar cheese instead of Monterey Jack.

2 cups water
1 cup long-grain rice, uncooked
¼ cup fat-free milk
⅛ teaspoon salt
1 (10¾-ounce) can reduced-sodium, reduced-fat cream of mushroom soup
1 (4.5-ounce) can chopped green chiles, drained
1½ cups (6 ounces) shredded reduced-fat Monterey Jack cheese, divided
Vegetable cooking spray
⅛ teaspoon paprika

Bring water to a boil in a saucepan. Stir in rice. Cover, reduce heat, and simmer 20 minutes or until rice is tender and liquid is absorbed. Add milk and next 3 ingredients; stir. Stir in 1 cup cheese.

Spoon mixture into an 11- x 7- x 1½-inch baking dish coated with cooking spray. Cover and bake at 350° for 30 minutes. Uncover and sprinkle with remaining ½ cup cheese and paprika. Bake, uncovered, 5 additional minutes. Yield: 8 (½-cup) servings.

PER SERVING: 175 CALORIES (27% FROM FAT)
FAT 5.2G (SATURATED FAT 2.7G)
PROTEIN 8.9G CARBOHYDRATE 22.8G
CHOLESTEROL 17MG SODIUM 374MG

ORANGE RICE PILAF

1 teaspoon olive oil
¼ cup chopped onion
1 cup long-grain rice, uncooked
1 cup canned reduced-sodium chicken broth
1 cup fresh orange juice
½ cup golden raisins
1 tablespoon grated orange rind
¼ teaspoon salt
¼ teaspoon freshly ground pepper

Heat oil in a medium nonstick skillet. Add onion; sauté until tender. Add rice; stir well. Cook, stirring constantly, 2 minutes. Add broth, juice, and raisins. Bring to a boil; cover, reduce heat, and simmer 20 to 25 minutes or until rice is tender and liquid is absorbed. Add orange rind, salt, and pepper; toss lightly. Yield: 5 (¾-cup) servings.

PER SERVING: 223 CALORIES (5% FROM FAT)
FAT 1.3G (SATURATED FAT 0.2G)
PROTEIN 3.8G CARBOHYDRATE 49.8G
CHOLESTEROL 0MG SODIUM 123MG

MEDITERRANEAN RICE PILAF

Vegetable cooking spray
1½ teaspoons reduced-calorie margarine
½ cup chopped onion
1 cup long-grain brown rice, uncooked
2½ cups canned reduced-sodium chicken broth
1 teaspoon ground coriander
¼ teaspoon salt
¼ teaspoon ground red pepper
¼ teaspoon ground turmeric
½ cup finely chopped fresh cilantro

Coat a large nonstick skillet with cooking spray; add margarine. Place over medium-high heat until margarine melts. Add onion; sauté 3 to 4 minutes or until tender. Add rice; cook, stirring constantly, 4 minutes or until rice is lightly browned.

Add broth and next 4 ingredients. Bring to a boil; cover, reduce heat, and simmer 40 minutes or until rice is tender and liquid is absorbed. Remove from heat, and stir in cilantro. Yield: 4 (¾-cup) servings.

PER SERVING: 204 CALORIES (12% FROM FAT)
FAT 2.6G (SATURATED FAT 0.4G)
PROTEIN 4.5G CARBOHYDRATE 39.0G
CHOLESTEROL 0MG SODIUM 172MG

MEXICAN RICE CAKES

1 (4.5-ounce) can chopped green chiles
2 cups cooked long-grain rice (cooked without salt or fat), chilled
1½ cups soft breadcrumbs
½ cup finely chopped tomato
2 tablespoons chopped fresh cilantro
1 teaspoon onion powder
1 teaspoon ground cumin
1 teaspoon chili powder
½ teaspoon garlic powder
½ teaspoon pepper
¼ teaspoon salt
2 egg whites, lightly beaten
Vegetable cooking spray
Fresh cilantro sprig (optional)
No-salt-added salsa (optional)

Drain chiles, and press firmly between paper towels to remove excess moisture. Combine chiles, rice, and next 10 ingredients in a bowl, stirring well. Shape rice mixture into 6 patties.

Coat a large nonstick skillet with cooking spray; place over medium heat until hot. Add rice patties, and cook 5 minutes on each side or until lightly browned.

Transfer patties to a serving platter. If desired, garnish with cilantro sprig and serve with salsa. Yield: 6 servings.

PER SERVING: 130 CALORIES (6% FROM FAT)
FAT 0.9G (SATURATED FAT 0.1G)
PROTEIN 4.2G CARBOHYDRATE 26.2G
CHOLESTEROL 0MG SODIUM 268MG

Mexican Rice Cakes

Curried Basmati Rice

CURRIED BASMATI RICE

If you're tired of plain white rice, here's a recipe to try soon. The basmati rice
has a nutty flavor that blends well with curry powder.

2 tablespoons reduced-calorie margarine
½ cup finely chopped onion
2 cloves garlic, minced
1½ cups basmati rice, uncooked
1 teaspoon curry powder
½ teaspoon salt
2 (10½-ounce) cans low-sodium chicken
    broth
½ cup water
¼ cup chopped fresh parsley
¼ teaspoon grated lemon rind
1 tablespoon fresh lemon juice

Melt margarine in a saucepan over medium heat. Add onion and garlic; sauté 5 minutes. Add rice and curry powder; cook, stirring constantly, 1 minute. Add salt, broth, and water; bring to a boil. Cover, reduce heat, and simmer 20 minutes or until liquid is absorbed. Remove from heat; stir in parsley, lemon rind, and lemon juice. Cover and let stand 10 minutes; fluff with a fork. Yield: 6 (1-cup) servings.

PER SERVING: 208 CALORIES (13% FROM FAT)
FAT 2.9G (SATURATED FAT 0.6G)
PROTEIN 4.7G CARBOHYDRATE 40.1G
CHOLESTEROL 0MG SODIUM 279MG

BASIC RISOTTO

4 (10½-ounce) cans low-sodium chicken broth
1 tablespoon olive oil
⅓ cup finely chopped onion
1½ cups Arborio rice or other short-grain rice,
    uncooked
⅓ cup dry white wine
½ teaspoon salt
¼ cup freshly grated Parmesan cheese

Bring broth to a simmer in a saucepan (do not boil). Keep broth warm over low heat.

Heat oil in a large saucepan over medium-high heat. Add onion; sauté 3 minutes. Add rice; cook, stirring constantly, 1 minute. Add wine and salt; cook, stirring constantly, 1 minute or until liquid is nearly absorbed. Add warm broth, ½ cup at a time, stirring constantly until each portion of broth is absorbed before adding next portion (about 20 minutes). Remove from heat; stir in cheese. Yield: 4 (1-cup) servings.

PER SERVING: 372 CALORIES (18% FROM FAT)
FAT 7.6G (SATURATED FAT 2.7G)
PROTEIN 10.6G   CARBOHYDRATE 64.1G
CHOLESTEROL 5MG   SODIUM 509MG

A Pearl of Wisdom

Risotto gets its classic creamy texture from plump, starchy rice. Arborio is the most readily available Italian rice that is exported to the United States, but you can also use medium- or short-grain American rice. The big difference is that Italian rice has a core (sometimes called the pearl) that remains firm to the bite, or *al dente*, while American-grown rice is a little more tender.

RISOTTO WITH SUN-DRIED TOMATOES AND BASIL

1 ounce sun-dried tomatoes (packed
    without oil)
½ cup boiling water
2 cups water
1 (14½-ounce) can vegetable broth
1 teaspoon olive oil
½ cup finely chopped shallot
1½ cups Arborio rice or other short-grain rice,
    uncooked
1 cup dry white wine
¾ cup freshly grated Parmesan cheese
½ cup thinly sliced fresh basil
⅛ teaspoon pepper
Shaved fresh Parmesan cheese (optional)
Fresh basil sprigs (optional)

Combine tomatoes and boiling water in a small bowl; cover and let stand 30 minutes or until softened. Drain and chop.

Combine 2 cups water and broth in a saucepan; bring to a simmer (do not boil). Keep warm.

Heat oil in a saucepan over medium heat. Add shallot; sauté 2 minutes. Stir in rice; sauté 5 minutes. Add wine; cook, stirring constantly, 1 minute or until wine is nearly absorbed.

Add broth mixture, ½ cup at a time, stirring often; cook until each portion of liquid is absorbed before adding next portion (about 25 minutes).

Add tomato; cook, stirring constantly, 2 minutes. Remove from heat; stir in ¾ cup cheese, sliced basil, and pepper. If desired, garnish with shaved Parmesan cheese and basil sprigs. Yield: 4 (1-cup) servings.

PER SERVING: 271 CALORIES (17% FROM FAT)
FAT 5.1G (SATURATED FAT 2.5G)
PROTEIN 9.6G   CARBOHYDRATE 46.2G
CHOLESTEROL 10MG   SODIUM 634MG

Wild Rice-Vegetable Medley

WILD RICE-VEGETABLE MEDLEY

For a quick and easy entrée, stir in 1 cup chopped cooked chicken.

Olive oil-flavored vegetable cooking spray
2 teaspoons olive oil
1 cup chopped green pepper
¾ cup chopped onion
¾ cup finely chopped carrot
1 (8-ounce) package sliced fresh mushrooms
1 (2¾-ounce) package instant wild rice, uncooked
1⅓ cups canned reduced-sodium chicken broth
¼ teaspoon salt
¼ teaspoon pepper
Fresh flat-leaf parsley leaves (optional)

Coat a saucepan with cooking spray; add oil. Place over medium-high heat until hot. Add chopped green pepper, onion, carrot, and mushrooms; sauté until carrot is tender.

Add rice and broth. Bring to a boil; reduce heat. Simmer, uncovered, 5 minutes or until liquid is absorbed. Stir in salt and pepper. Let stand 5 minutes. Garnish with fresh parsley leaves, if desired. Yield: 5 (¾-cup) servings.

PER SERVING: 157 CALORIES (15% FROM FAT)
FAT 2.6G (SATURATED FAT 0.3G)
PROTEIN 4.1G   CARBOHYDRATE 22.4G
CHOLESTEROL 0MG   SODIUM 128MG

ASIAN COUSCOUS

Vegetable cooking spray
½ cup sliced green onions
1½ cups water
2 tablespoons low-sodium soy sauce
½ teaspoon sugar
¼ teaspoon ground ginger
¼ teaspoon garlic powder
¼ teaspoon ground red pepper
1 cup couscous, uncooked

Place a saucepan coated with cooking spray over medium-high heat until hot. Add green onions, and sauté until tender.

Add water and next 5 ingredients; bring to a boil. Remove from heat.

Add couscous to pan; cover and let stand 5 minutes or until couscous is tender and liquid is absorbed. Fluff with a fork; transfer to a serving bowl. Yield: 6 (½-cup) servings.

PER SERVING: 131 CALORIES (1% FROM FAT)
FAT 0.1G (SATURATED FAT 0.0G)
PROTEIN 4.5G   CARBOHYDRATE 26.9G
CHOLESTEROL 0MG   SODIUM 132MG

Introducing Couscous

Few pastas or grains are easier to prepare than couscous. A popular cereal in North Africa, couscous (KOOS-koos) is a bland beadlike pasta that takes on flavors easily. Season it and serve it simply as you would rice or pasta, toss it with a fragrant dressing for a salad, or sweeten it and mix with fruit. You'll find couscous in boxes on the pasta or rice aisle of the supermarket.

GARDEN ORZO

Orzo is a small rice-shaped pasta that's not much larger than a pine nut. For a change, cook orzo rather than rice for dinner.

½ pound fresh asparagus
1½ quarts water
1 cup orzo, uncooked
Vegetable cooking spray
1 teaspoon olive oil
¾ cup sliced carrot
1 clove garlic, minced
1 cup sliced fresh mushrooms
¼ cup water
½ teaspoon chicken-flavored bouillon granules
½ teaspoon grated lemon rind
¼ teaspoon salt
¼ teaspoon pepper
¼ cup grated Asiago cheese
Lemon slices (optional)

Snap off tough ends of asparagus. Remove scales from stalks with a knife or vegetable peeler, if desired. Cut asparagus into 1-inch pieces.

Bring 1½ quarts water to a boil in a large saucepan. Add orzo, and cook 5 minutes. Add asparagus, and cook 4 additional minutes or until orzo is tender; drain well. Place orzo and asparagus in a serving bowl. Set aside, and keep warm.

Coat a large nonstick skillet with cooking spray; add oil. Place over medium-high heat until hot. Add carrot and garlic; sauté until carrot is crisp-tender. Add mushrooms, and sauté until tender.

Combine ¼ cup water and next 4 ingredients; add to carrot mixture. Bring to a boil, and cook 1 minute. Add carrot mixture and cheese to orzo mixture; toss gently. Garnish with lemon slices, if desired. Yield: 9 (½-cup) servings.

PER SERVING: 107 CALORIES (14% FROM FAT)
FAT 1.7G (SATURATED FAT 0.5G)
PROTEIN 4.5G   CARBOHYDRATE 18.7G
CHOLESTEROL 2MG   SODIUM 156MG

ASIAN NOODLES

3 quarts water
1 (7-ounce) package rice vermicelli, uncooked
3 tablespoons low-sodium soy sauce
2 tablespoons honey
2 teaspoons dark sesame oil, divided
Vegetable cooking spray
1 cup diagonally sliced green onions
1 tablespoon peeled, minced gingerroot
1 teaspoon toasted sesame seeds

Bring water to a boil in a large saucepan; add pasta, and cook 3 minutes or until tender. Drain. Place pasta in a serving bowl, and keep warm.

Combine soy sauce, honey, and 1 teaspoon oil; stir well. Add soy sauce mixture to pasta; toss well.

Coat a nonstick skillet with cooking spray; add remaining 1 teaspoon oil. Place over medium-high heat until hot. Add green onions and gingerroot; sauté 1 minute. Add onion mixture to pasta mixture; toss lightly. Sprinkle with sesame seeds just before serving. Yield: 8 (¾-cup) servings.

PER SERVING: 224 CALORIES (13% FROM FAT)
FAT 3.2G (SATURATED FAT 0.7G)
PROTEIN 4.5G   CARBOHYDRATE 44.3G
CHOLESTEROL 0MG   SODIUM 149MG

Know Your Noodles

Rice vermicelli is a type of noodle made from rice flour. It's also called long rice, Chinese vermicelli, and rice sticks.

CREAMY MACARONI AND CHEESE

For a hearty one-dish meal, stir in 2 cups cubed reduced-fat, low-salt ham.

1 (8-ounce) package elbow macaroni, uncooked
2 tablespoons reduced-calorie margarine
2 cups frozen chopped onion, celery, and pepper blend, thawed
2½ cups low-fat milk
¼ cup all-purpose flour
1¼ cups (5 ounces) shredded reduced-fat sharp Cheddar cheese, divided
½ teaspoon salt
¼ teaspoon pepper
Vegetable cooking spray

Cook pasta according to package directions, omitting salt and fat; drain. Set aside, and keep warm.

Melt margarine in a large saucepan over medium-high heat. Add vegetables; sauté until tender. Reduce heat to medium. Combine milk and flour, stirring until smooth. Add milk mixture to vegetable mixture. Cook, stirring constantly, 10 to 15 minutes or until thickened and bubbly. Remove from heat. Add 1 cup cheese, salt, and pepper, stirring until cheese melts. Add macaroni to cheese mixture; stir well.

Spoon macaroni mixture into a 1½-quart baking dish coated with cooking spray. Sprinkle with remaining ¼ cup cheese. Cover and bake at 375° for 15 to 20 minutes or until bubbly. Let stand 10 minutes before serving. Yield: 8 (¾-cup) servings.

PER SERVING: 231 CALORIES (26% FROM FAT)
FAT 6.6G (SATURATED FAT 2.8G)
PROTEIN 12.2G   CARBOHYDRATE 30.6G
CHOLESTEROL 15MG   SODIUM 352MG

Tangy Dijon Pasta

TANGY DIJON PASTA

2 cups fresh snow pea pods
¼ cup plus 2 tablespoons low-fat sour
   cream
3 tablespoons dry white wine
2 tablespoons Dijon mustard
4 ounces capellini (angel hair pasta),
   uncooked
Vegetable cooking spray
½ cup diced purple onion
1 (2-ounce) jar sliced pimiento, drained

Wash peas; trim ends, and remove strings. Cook, uncovered, in a small amount of boiling water 3 minutes. Drain; set aside, and keep warm.

Combine sour cream, wine, and mustard in a bowl; stir well with a wire whisk, and set aside.

Cook pasta according to package directions, omitting salt and fat. Drain and set aside.

Coat a large skillet with cooking spray; place over medium-high heat until hot. Add onion; sauté 2 to 3 minutes or until tender. Add peas, sour cream mixture, pasta, and pimiento. Cook, stirring constantly, 2 to 3 minutes or until thoroughly heated. Serve immediately. Yield: 7 (½-cup) servings.

PER SERVING: 102 CALORIES (20% FROM FAT)
FAT 2.3G (SATURATED FAT 1.0G)
PROTEIN 3.4G CARBOHYDRATE 16.5G
CHOLESTEROL 5MG SODIUM 137MG

HOT SESAME SPAGHETTI

*Save time by purchasing broccoli flowerets in the produce section or chopped
broccoli and red pepper from the salad bar.*

8 ounces spaghetti, uncooked
2 teaspoons hot chile oil, divided
Vegetable cooking spray
2½ cups coarsely chopped broccoli flowerets
1 cup diced sweet red pepper
½ cup chopped green onions
1½ teaspoons minced garlic
1 tablespoon sesame seeds, lightly toasted
½ teaspoon salt

Cook spaghetti according to package directions,
omitting salt and fat; drain well. Toss spaghetti
with 1 teaspoon hot chile oil, and keep warm.

Coat a large nonstick skillet with cooking spray;
add remaining 1 teaspoon oil. Place over medium-
high heat until hot.

Add broccoli, sweet red pepper, green onions,
and garlic to skillet; sauté until vegetables are
crisp-tender.

Add broccoli mixture, toasted sesame seeds, and
salt to spaghetti; toss mixture well. Yield: 6 (1-cup)
servings.

PER SERVING: 181 CALORIES (15% FROM FAT)
FAT 3.1G (SATURATED FAT 0.5G)
PROTEIN 6.5G   CARBOHYDRATE 32.2G
CHOLESTEROL 0MG   SODIUM 209MG

Hot Sesame Spaghetti

ORECCHIETTE WITH FRESH VEGETABLES AND HERBS

(pictured on page 92)

12 ounces orecchiette (bowl-shaped pasta),
      uncooked
10 ounces fresh asparagus
1 (14½-ounce) can vegetable broth
1½ cups julienne-sliced sweet yellow pepper
1 cup diagonally sliced carrot
2 cups Sugar Snap peas, trimmed
1 cup frozen English peas
¼ cup chopped fresh chives
2 tablespoons chopped fresh basil
1 tablespoon chopped fresh thyme
⅛ teaspoon salt
¾ cup grated Romano cheese
Freshly ground pepper (optional)
Fresh basil sprigs (optional)

Cook pasta according to package directions, omitting salt and fat; drain well. Place pasta in a serving bowl; keep warm.

Snap off tough ends of asparagus. Remove scales from stalks with a knife or vegetable peeler, if desired. Cut asparagus into 1-inch pieces.

Bring broth to a boil in a large saucepan. Add asparagus, yellow pepper, and carrot. Reduce heat; simmer, uncovered, 4 minutes. Add Sugar Snap and English peas; cook 3 additional minutes or until vegetables are crisp-tender. Add chives and next 3 ingredients.

Add vegetable mixture to pasta; toss well. Add ½ cup cheese, and toss well. Sprinkle with remaining ¼ cup cheese and, if desired, freshly ground pepper. Garnish with fresh basil, if desired. Yield: 8 (¾-cup) servings.

PER SERVING: 241 CALORIES (15% FROM FAT)
FAT 3.9G (SATURATED FAT 1.9G)
PROTEIN 11.2G   CARBOHYDRATE 40.6G
CHOLESTEROL 11MG   SODIUM 350MG

PASTA PRIMAVERA

(pictured on cover)

Chop the bright green, feathery foliage, or fronds, on the fennel bulb to add a subtle licorice flavor to this dish.

2 cups diagonally sliced carrot
2 cups cavatappi (spiral-shaped tubular pasta),
      uncooked
1½ tablespoons olive oil
1 cup chopped fennel bulb
1½ cups thinly sliced leek (about 1 medium)
½ cup sweet red pepper strips
½ cup sweet yellow pepper strips
¼ cup chopped fresh basil
2 tablespoons chopped fresh dillweed
2 tablespoons chopped fresh thyme
3 cloves garlic, minced
1 cup Sugar Snap peas, trimmed
½ cup dry vermouth
½ teaspoon salt
¾ cup grated Asiago cheese
2 tablespoons chopped fennel fronds

Arrange carrot in a steamer basket over boiling water. Cover and steam 5 minutes or until crisp-tender. Set aside.

Cook pasta according to package directions, omitting salt and fat; drain well. Set aside; keep warm.

Heat oil in a large nonstick skillet over medium-high heat. Add chopped fennel bulb, and sauté 3 minutes.

Add leek and next 6 ingredients; sauté 5 minutes. Add carrot, peas, vermouth, and salt. Cover, reduce heat, and simmer 2 minutes.

Combine pasta, vegetable mixture, ½ cup cheese, and fennel fronds in a large bowl; toss well. Sprinkle with remaining ¼ cup cheese. Yield: 8 (1-cup) servings.

PER SERVING: 221 CALORIES (24% FROM FAT)
FAT 6.0G (SATURATED FAT 2.2G)
PROTEIN 9.6G   CARBOHYDRATE 32.1G
CHOLESTEROL 7MG   SODIUM 357MG

ROASTED VEGETABLES WITH GEMELLI

Gemelli, a rope-shaped pasta, adds a special twist to this dish. If it's not available, substitute fusilli.

1 large zucchini
1 large yellow squash
1 large sweet red pepper
1 (8-ounce) package fresh mushrooms
1 large onion, cut into thin wedges
2 tablespoons balsamic vinegar
2 teaspoons olive oil
½ teaspoon dried rosemary
½ teaspoon sugar
¼ teaspoon salt
¼ teaspoon freshly ground pepper
2 large tomatoes, coarsely chopped
10 ounces gemelli (rope-shaped pasta), uncooked
2 ounces crumbled goat cheese
¼ cup shredded fresh basil
Freshly ground pepper (optional)

Line a 15- x 10- x 1-inch jellyroll pan with aluminum foil; set aside. Cut zucchini, squash, and red pepper into 1-inch pieces. Place on prepared pan; add mushrooms and onion.

Combine vinegar and next 5 ingredients in a small bowl; stir well. Brush over vegetables in pan. Bake at 425° for 15 minutes. Stir vegetables, and add tomato. Bake 10 additional minutes or until vegetables are tender and golden.

Cook pasta according to package directions, omitting salt and fat; drain. Place pasta in a serving bowl. Add roasted vegetables; toss well. Top with goat cheese and basil. Sprinkle with freshly ground pepper, if desired. Yield: 10 (1-cup) servings.

PER SERVING: 160 CALORIES (16% FROM FAT)
FAT 2.9G (SATURATED FAT 1.1G)
PROTEIN 6.1G CARBOHYDRATE 28.3G
CHOLESTEROL 5MG SODIUM 130MG

RIGATONI WITH SWEET PEPPERS, OLIVES, AND FETA

Kalamata olives—dark purple, almond-shaped olives imported from Greece—are used in this Mediterranean-style recipe. Although you can substitute black olives, if desired, their flavor will not be as rich and fruity.

1 pound rigatoni, uncooked
¼ cup chopped kalamata olives (about 16)
1 tablespoon chopped fresh oregano or
    1 teaspoon dried oregano
¼ teaspoon salt
⅛ teaspoon dried crushed red pepper
2 teaspoons olive oil
2 cups thinly sliced onion
4 cloves garlic, minced
2 cups sweet red pepper strips
2 cups green pepper strips
½ cup water
¾ cup crumbled feta cheese

Cook pasta according to package directions, omitting salt and fat; drain. Set aside, and keep warm.

Combine olives and next 3 ingredients; set aside.

Heat oil in a large nonstick skillet over medium-high heat. Add onion, and sauté 3 minutes or until tender. Add garlic; cook 1 minute. Stir in pepper strips. Cover; reduce heat, and cook 10 minutes.

Add ½ cup water; cover and simmer 10 additional minutes or until pepper strips are tender. Stir in olive mixture.

Combine pepper mixture and pasta in a large bowl; toss well. Add feta cheese; toss gently. Yield: 8 (1-cup) servings.

PER SERVING: 216 CALORIES (20% FROM FAT)
FAT 4.8G (SATURATED FAT 2.0G)
PROTEIN 7.4G CARBOHYDRATE 36.2G
CHOLESTEROL 9MG SODIUM 227MG

Rigatoni with Sweet Peppers, Olives, and Feta

Stewed Okra, Corn, and Tomatoes (recipe on page 120)

VERSATILE VEGETABLES

Flavor, texture, and nutrients—what valuable traits describe this one group of foods! Add versatility and ease of preparation and you have a meal component not to be ignored. To maintain the vegetable's natural goodness and keep fat to a minimum, simply follow one of these basic cooking techniques.

Stir-fry, roast, grill, steam, or sauté your favorite vegetables, and you'll see how fresh they can taste. For instance, Green Beans Provençale (page 113) calls for green beans to be steamed; the result is beans with fresh taste, lots of texture, and maximum nutrients. And the mixed vegetables in Quick "Roasted" Succotash (page 114) take on a smoky flavor when sautéed over high heat.

Use herbs and spices instead of fat to season vegetable side dishes; Basil-Wrapped Corn on the Cob (page 117) and Pan-Fried Dill Tomatoes (page 126) are two tasty examples. Turn to pages 9 and 10 for more about specific cooking directions and vegetable-herb combinations.

Nutty Asparagus

NUTTY ASPARAGUS

1 pound fresh asparagus spears
Vegetable cooking spray
1 tablespoon lemon juice
2 teaspoons reduced-calorie margarine, melted
1 tablespoon coarsely chopped walnuts
¼ teaspoon salt
⅛ teaspoon freshly ground pepper

Snap off tough ends of asparagus. Remove scales from stalks with a knife or vegetable peeler, if desired. Place asparagus in an 8-inch square baking dish coated with cooking spray.

Combine lemon juice and margarine; brush over asparagus. Sprinkle with walnuts, salt, and pepper. Bake, uncovered, at 350° for 20 minutes or until asparagus is tender. Yield: 4 servings.

PER SERVING: 44 CALORIES (55% FROM FAT)
FAT 2.7G (SATURATED FAT 0.3G)
PROTEIN 2.4G   CARBOHYDRATE 4.5G
CHOLESTEROL 0MG   SODIUM 167MG

ASPARAGUS WITH CREAMY CHIVE SAUCE

1 pound fresh asparagus spears
½ cup plain nonfat yogurt
2 tablespoons fat-free milk
4 ounces nonfat cream cheese
2 tablespoons freeze-dried chives
¼ teaspoon salt
⅛ teaspoon garlic powder
⅛ teaspoon pepper

Snap off tough ends of asparagus. Remove scales from stalks with a knife or vegetable peeler, if desired. Arrange asparagus in a steamer basket over boiling water. Cover and steam 7 minutes or until crisp-tender; drain. Transfer to a serving platter; set aside, and keep warm.

Combine yogurt, milk, and cream cheese in a small saucepan, stirring well with a wire whisk. Place over medium-high heat; cook, stirring constantly, 5 minutes or until cheese melts and mixture is thoroughly heated. Remove from heat.

Stir chives and remaining 3 ingredients into yogurt mixture. Pour yogurt mixture over asparagus. Yield: 6 servings.

PER SERVING: 43 CALORIES (4% FROM FAT)
FAT 0.2G (SATURATED FAT 0.1G)
PROTEIN 5.5G   CARBOHYDRATE 5.0G
CHOLESTEROL 4MG   SODIUM 234MG

GREEN BEANS WITH LEMON AND GARLIC

¾ cup water
1 pound fresh green beans, trimmed
2½ teaspoons olive oil
3 cloves garlic, minced
3 tablespoons fresh lemon juice
⅛ teaspoon salt
⅛ teaspoon pepper

Bring water to a boil in a large nonstick skillet; add beans. Cook 3 minutes; drain.

Heat oil in skillet over medium-high heat. Add garlic and beans; sauté 1 minute. Add lemon juice, salt, and pepper, tossing gently; sauté 1 minute. Yield: 4 (1-cup) servings.

PER SERVING: 66 CALORIES (40% FROM FAT)
FAT 2.9G (SATURATED FAT 0.4G)
PROTEIN 2.3G   CARBOHYDRATE 9.9G
CHOLESTEROL 0MG   SODIUM 78MG

GREEN BEANS PROVENÇALE

2 pounds fresh green beans, cut into 1½-inch
    pieces
24 small cherry tomatoes, halved
½ cup chopped purple onion
¾ cup chopped fresh parsley
¼ cup water
¼ cup white wine vinegar
2 tablespoons grated Parmesan cheese
2 tablespoons olive oil
½ teaspoon dried thyme
½ teaspoon pepper
2 cloves garlic, minced

Arrange beans in a steamer basket over boiling water. Cover and steam 8 minutes or until crisp-tender. Drain beans; plunge into cold water, and drain. Combine beans, tomatoes, and onion in a serving bowl.

Combine parsley and remaining 7 ingredients, stirring until well blended. Pour over vegetables, tossing gently to coat. Serve at room temperature. Yield: 12 (1-cup) servings.

PER SERVING: 56 CALORIES (42% FROM FAT)
FAT 2.6G (SATURATED FAT 0.5G)
PROTEIN 2.0G   CARBOHYDRATE 7.2G
CHOLESTEROL 0MG   SODIUM 25MG

Quick "Roasted" Succotash

QUICK "ROASTED" SUCCOTASH

*Cooking the mixed vegetables over high heat gives them a robust, smoky flavor
similar to that of oven-roasted vegetables.*

1½ cups fresh corn kernels (about 3 ears)
1 cup chopped sweet red pepper
½ cup chopped onion
1 teaspoon ground cumin
1 cup chopped yellow squash
1½ tablespoons olive oil
2 cloves garlic, minced
½ cup low-sodium chicken broth
2 tablespoons chopped fresh cilantro
½ teaspoon salt
⅛ teaspoon pepper
⅛ teaspoon hot sauce
1 (10-ounce) package frozen baby lima beans,
   thawed

Place a large nonstick skillet over high heat until hot. Add first 4 ingredients; sauté 5 minutes or until vegetables are slightly blackened. Add squash, oil, and garlic; sauté over medium-high heat 1 minute. Add broth and remaining ingredients; cook 5 minutes or until thoroughly heated, stirring often.
Yield: 5 (1-cup) servings.

PER SERVING: 170 CALORIES (28% FROM FAT)
FAT 5.2G (SATURATED FAT 0.7G)
PROTEIN 6.9G CARBOHYDRATE 26.8G
CHOLESTEROL 0MG SODIUM 337MG

Bok Choy with Ginger and Water Chestnuts

Follow these bok choy basics: pull off ragged or discolored leaves; then slice the leaves across the rib.

Vegetable cooking spray
1 teaspoon sesame oil
1¼ pounds bok choy, trimmed and sliced
½ cup thinly sliced green onions
1 teaspoon peeled, grated gingerroot
2 cloves garlic, minced
1 (8-ounce) can sliced water chestnuts, drained
3 tablespoons low-sodium soy sauce

Coat a large nonstick skillet with cooking spray; add oil. Place over medium-high heat until hot. Add bok choy and next 3 ingredients; cover and cook 5 minutes, stirring once.

Add water chestnuts and soy sauce to skillet; cook 1 minute. Yield: 4 (¾-cup) servings.

PER SERVING: 59 CALORIES (24% FROM FAT)
FAT 1.6G (SATURATED FAT 0.2G)
PROTEIN 2.8G   CARBOHYDRATE 9.0G
CHOLESTEROL 0MG   SODIUM 390MG

Broccoli with Dijon Vinaigrette

2 pounds fresh broccoli spears
1 tablespoon plus 1 teaspoon olive oil
¼ cup finely chopped green onions
½ teaspoon dried tarragon
½ teaspoon dry mustard
3 cloves garlic, minced
2 tablespoons red wine vinegar
2 tablespoons water
1 tablespoon Dijon mustard
¼ teaspoon pepper
⅛ teaspoon salt

Arrange broccoli in a steamer basket over boiling water. Cover and steam 6 minutes or until crisp-tender. Drain; place in a serving bowl.

Heat oil in a small saucepan over medium heat. Add green onions and next 3 ingredients; sauté 3 minutes. Remove from heat; add vinegar and remaining 4 ingredients, stirring with a wire whisk until blended. Drizzle over broccoli, tossing gently to coat. Yield: 8 servings.

PER SERVING: 58 CALORIES (43% FROM FAT)
FAT 2.8G (SATURATED FAT 0.4G)
PROTEIN 3.6G   CARBOHYDRATE 6.9G
CHOLESTEROL 0MG   SODIUM 122MG

Broccoli Casserole

It takes about 2 slices of whole wheat bread to make 1 cup of soft breadcrumbs.

2 (10-ounce) packages frozen chopped broccoli
1 (10¾-ounce) can reduced-fat, reduced-sodium cream of celery (or mushroom) soup
1 (8-ounce) can sliced water chestnuts, drained
1 (4-ounce) can sliced mushrooms, drained
¼ teaspoon salt
⅛ teaspoon pepper
Vegetable cooking spray
1 cup soft whole wheat breadcrumbs
⅔ cup (2.6 ounces) shredded reduced-fat sharp Cheddar cheese
1 tablespoon reduced-calorie margarine, melted

Cook broccoli according to package directions; drain. Combine broccoli, soup, and next 4 ingredients. Spoon mixture into a 1½-quart baking dish coated with cooking spray.

Combine breadcrumbs, cheese, and margarine. Sprinkle crumb mixture over broccoli mixture. Bake, uncovered, at 350° for 30 minutes. Yield: 8 servings.

PER SERVING: 112 CALORIES (31% FROM FAT)
FAT 3.8G (SATURATED FAT 1.4G)
PROTEIN 6.3G   CARBOHYDRATE 14.8G
CHOLESTEROL 7MG   SODIUM 378MG

Sweet-and-Sour Cabbage with Vidalias

*The sweet-sour flavor of this dish complements
entrées such as pot roast or pork.*

1 tablespoon olive oil
7½ cups vertically sliced Vidalia onion
8 cups thinly sliced napa (Chinese) cabbage
3¼ cups seeded, chopped tomato
¼ cup white wine vinegar
1 teaspoon salt
¼ teaspoon pepper
2 tablespoons sugar

Heat oil in an 8-quart stockpot or Dutch oven
over medium-high heat. Add onion; sauté 5 minutes or until tender. Add cabbage and next 4 ingredients; cook 10 minutes or until cabbage is tender,
stirring often. Stir in sugar; cook 1 minute. Serve
with pot roast or pork. Yield: 7 (1-cup) servings.

PER SERVING: 107 CALORIES (22% FROM FAT)
FAT 2.6G (SATURATED FAT 0.4G)
PROTEIN 3.3G   CARBOHYDRATE 19.9G
CHOLESTEROL 0MG   SODIUM 399MG

Marbled Carrots and Parsnips

3 cups sliced carrot (about 1 pound)
4 cups water, divided
3 cups sliced parsnip (about 1 pound)
1 cup fat-free milk, divided
1 tablespoon plus 1 teaspoon reduced-calorie
    margarine, divided
½ teaspoon vanilla extract
2 teaspoons sugar
¼ teaspoon salt

Combine carrot and 2 cups water in a saucepan.
Bring to a boil; cover, reduce heat, and simmer 35
minutes or until very tender. Drain; set carrot aside.
Combine parsnip and remaining 2 cups water in
saucepan. Bring to a boil; cover, reduce heat, and
simmer 20 minutes or until very tender. Drain well,
and set parsnip aside.
Position knife blade in food processor bowl; add
carrot, ½ cup milk, 2 teaspoons margarine, and
vanilla. Process until smooth; pour mixture into
saucepan. Cook over medium-low heat 5 minutes
or until thoroughly heated, stirring occasionally; set
carrot mixture aside.
Rinse and dry food processor bowl and knife
blade. Position knife blade in food processor bowl;
add parsnip, remaining ½ cup milk, remaining 2
teaspoons margarine, sugar, and salt. Process until
smooth. Pour mixture into a saucepan, and cook
over medium-low heat 5 minutes or until thoroughly heated.
Spoon carrot mixture into half of a small serving bowl, and spoon parsnip mixture into other
half. Pull a small rubber spatula through mixtures
to create a marbled pattern. Yield: 4 (1-cup)
servings.

PER SERVING: 169 CALORIES (13% FROM FAT)
FAT 2.4G (SATURATED FAT 0.4G)
PROTEIN 4.3G   CARBOHYDRATE 34.0G
CHOLESTEROL 1MG   SODIUM 265MG

Lime-Glazed Carrots

1 pound carrots, scraped and cut diagonally
    into ¼-inch slices
½ cup water
1 tablespoon sugar
1½ tablespoons fresh lime juice
2 teaspoons margarine
¼ teaspoon salt

Cook carrot in a small amount of boiling water in
a saucepan 4 minutes or until crisp-tender; drain
and return to pan. Add ½ cup water and sugar;
bring to a boil. Reduce heat; simmer, uncovered,
9 minutes or until liquid evaporates and carrot is
tender. Stir in lime juice, margarine, and salt.
Yield: 3 (½-cup) servings.

PER SERVING: 81 CALORIES (30% FROM FAT)
FAT 2.7G (SATURATED FAT 0.5G)
PROTEIN 1.0G   CARBOHYDRATE 14.5G
CHOLESTEROL 0MG   SODIUM 258MG

CAULIFLOWER WITH PIMIENTO-OLIVE VINAIGRETTE

4½ cups cauliflower flowerets
½ cup reduced-sodium chicken broth
¼ cup sliced pimiento-stuffed olives
1 tablespoon lemon juice
1 tablespoon white wine vinegar
2 teaspoons olive oil
½ teaspoon dried oregano
¼ teaspoon salt
¼ teaspoon pepper
1 (2-ounce) jar diced pimiento, drained
1 clove garlic, crushed

Arrange cauliflower in a steamer basket over boiling water. Cover and steam 8 minutes or until crisp-tender. Transfer to a serving bowl; set aside, and keep warm.

Combine broth and remaining 9 ingredients in a small saucepan; bring to a boil. Pour over cauliflower; toss gently. Yield: 4 (1-cup) servings.

PER SERVING: 62 CALORIES (46% FROM FAT)
FAT 3.2G (SATURATED FAT 0.5G)
PROTEIN 2.5G   CARBOHYDRATE 7.3G
CHOLESTEROL 0MG   SODIUM 260MG

BASIL-WRAPPED CORN ON THE COB

(pictured on page 2)

4 ears fresh corn
2 teaspoons reduced-calorie margarine, melted
¼ teaspoon salt
¼ teaspoon freshly ground pepper
24 large fresh basil leaves

Remove husks and silks from corn. Combine margarine, salt, and pepper in a small bowl, stirring well. Brush margarine mixture over corn. Place each ear on a piece of heavy-duty aluminum foil. Place 3 basil leaves under each ear of corn and 3

leaves over each ear. Roll foil lengthwise around each ear; twist at ends to seal.

Place foil-wrapped corn on a baking sheet. Bake at 450° for 15 minutes or until tender. Yield: 4 servings.

PER SERVING: 106 CALORIES (20% FROM FAT)
FAT 2.4G (SATURATED FAT 0.3G)
PROTEIN 3.1G   CARBOHYDRATE 22.1G
CHOLESTEROL 0MG   SODIUM 180MG

EASY CORN CASSEROLE

¼ cup fat-free egg substitute
¼ cup reduced-calorie stick margarine, melted
1 (8¾-ounce) can no-salt-added whole-kernel corn, drained
1 (8¾-ounce) can no-salt-added cream-style corn
1 (8½-ounce) package corn muffin mix
1 (8-ounce) carton plain nonfat yogurt
Vegetable cooking spray

Combine first 6 ingredients; stir well. Pour into an 8-inch square baking dish coated with cooking spray. Bake, uncovered, at 350° for 45 minutes or until set. Yield: 8 servings.

PER SERVING: 220 CALORIES (31% FROM FAT)
FAT 7.5G (SATURATED FAT 2.5G)
PROTEIN 5.4G   CARBOHYDRATE 34.6G
CHOLESTEROL 1MG   SODIUM 287MG

Easy Corn Casserole

ITALIAN EGGPLANT CASSEROLE

1½ pounds eggplant (about 2 small)
¼ cup canned reduced-sodium chicken broth
¾ cup sliced fresh mushrooms
½ cup chopped onion
½ cup chopped celery
¼ cup chopped green onions
¼ cup chopped green pepper
¼ cup no-salt-added tomato paste
2 tablespoons chopped fresh parsley
¾ teaspoon minced fresh thyme or
    ¼ teaspoon dried thyme
¾ teaspoon minced fresh oregano or
    ¼ teaspoon dried oregano
½ teaspoon pepper
¼ teaspoon hot sauce
2 (8-ounce) cans no-salt-added tomato sauce
Vegetable cooking spray
½ cup (2 ounces) shredded part-skim
    mozzarella cheese
2 tablespoons freshly grated Parmesan cheese

Cut eggplant into ¼-inch-thick slices. Arrange eggplant, in batches, in a steamer basket over boiling water. Cover and steam 8 to 10 minutes or until tender. Drain on paper towels, and set aside.

Heat broth in a large saucepan over medium-high heat until hot. Add mushrooms and next 4 ingredients. Sauté until vegetables are tender. Remove from heat; add tomato paste and next 6 ingredients, stirring well.

Arrange half of eggplant slices in an 11- x 7- x 1½-inch baking dish coated with cooking spray. Spoon half of tomato mixture over eggplant, and sprinkle ¼ cup mozzarella cheese over tomato mixture. Repeat layers. Sprinkle with Parmesan cheese. Bake, uncovered, at 350° for 30 minutes or until thoroughly heated. Yield: 8 servings.

PER SERVING: 81 CALORIES (20% FROM FAT)
FAT 1.8G (SATURATED FAT 1.0G)
PROTEIN 4.5G CARBOHYDRATE 13.1G
CHOLESTEROL 5MG SODIUM 89MG

GRATIN OF LEEKS

The leeks in this dish become soft and mellow-flavored during baking.

6 cups water
8 medium leeks (about 3 pounds), trimmed
    and cleaned
2 cups low-fat milk
½ teaspoon dried thyme
¼ teaspoon ground nutmeg
4 whole cloves
1 bay leaf
1 clove garlic, minced
¼ cup all-purpose flour
2 tablespoons dry white wine
1 tablespoon margarine
½ cup (2 ounces) grated Gruyère or Swiss
    cheese
Vegetable cooking spray
2 tablespoons grated Parmesan cheese
⅛ teaspoon ground red pepper

Bring water to a boil in a Dutch oven; add leeks. Cover and cook 8 minutes or until tender; drain well, and pat leeks dry with paper towels. Set aside.

Combine milk and next 5 ingredients in a medium saucepan. Bring to a boil over medium heat; boil, stirring constantly, 1 minute. Remove from heat, and cool. Pour through a wire-mesh strainer into a bowl, discarding solids.

Place flour in saucepan. Gradually add milk mixture, stirring with a wire whisk until blended. Bring mixture to a boil; reduce heat, and simmer, uncovered, 2 minutes or until thickened, stirring constantly.

Add wine and margarine; cook, stirring constantly, 1 minute or until margarine melts. Remove from heat; add Gruyère cheese, stirring until melted.

Arrange leeks in an 11- x 7- x 1½-inch baking dish coated with cooking spray. Pour milk mixture over leeks; sprinkle with Parmesan cheese and pepper. Bake, uncovered, at 400° for 25 minutes or until lightly browned. Yield: 8 servings.

PER SERVING: 165 CALORIES (28% FROM FAT)
FAT 5.2G (SATURATED FAT 2.3G)
PROTEIN 6.9G CARBOHYDRATE 23.3G
CHOLESTEROL 11MG SODIUM 119MG

Gratin of Leeks

HEARTY LENTIL POTPOURRI

1 (14¼-ounce) can reduced-sodium beef
    broth
1 cup chopped carrot
¾ cup chopped celery
¾ cup chopped onion
¾ cup frozen whole-kernel corn,
    thawed
½ cup dried lentils, uncooked
1 tablespoon low-sodium soy sauce
½ teaspoon ground coriander
¼ teaspoon dried basil
¼ teaspoon dried marjoram
¼ teaspoon dried thyme
⅛ teaspoon pepper
2 cloves garlic, minced
¼ teaspoon salt

Combine all ingredients except salt in a Dutch
oven. Bring to a boil; cover, reduce heat, and
simmer 40 minutes or until lentils and vegetables
are tender. Stir in salt; serve immediately. Yield:
5 (¾-cup) servings.

PER SERVING: 78 CALORIES (5% FROM FAT)
FAT 0.4G (SATURATED FAT 0.1G)
PROTEIN 3.9G   CARBOHYDRATE 14.7G
CHOLESTEROL 0MG   SODIUM 225MG

STEWED OKRA, CORN, AND TOMATOES

(pictured on page 110)

1½ cups frozen sliced okra
1 cup frozen whole-kernel corn
¼ cup chopped reduced-fat, low-salt
    cooked ham
1 teaspoon dried basil
¼ teaspoon salt
¼ teaspoon pepper
1 (14½-ounce) can no-salt-added stewed
    tomatoes, undrained
Vegetable cooking spray

Combine first 7 ingredients in a large saucepan
coated with cooking spray. Bring to a boil; cover,
reduce heat, and simmer 15 minutes, stirring occasionally. Yield: 4 (¾-cup) servings.

PER SERVING: 88 CALORIES (8% FROM FAT)
FAT 0.8G (SATURATED FAT 0.2G)
PROTEIN 4.7G   CARBOHYDRATE 17.7G
CHOLESTEROL 4MG   SODIUM 238MG

GRILLED BALSAMIC ONIONS WITH PINEAPPLE CHUTNEY

2 large onions (about 1½ pounds)
Vegetable cooking spray
¼ cup mango chutney
¼ cup drained, crushed pineapple in juice
3 tablespoons balsamic vinegar, divided

Peel onions, and slice each into 4 slices. Place
onion slices in a single layer in a 13- x 9- x 2-inch
baking dish coated with cooking spray. Cover and
microwave at HIGH 5 minutes.
  Combine chutney and pineapple; set aside.
  Remove onion slices from dish, and place in
a single layer on 2 large pieces of aluminum foil
coated with cooking spray. Brush onion slices
evenly with half of vinegar; wrap tightly in aluminum foil.
  Place foil packets, seam sides down, on grill rack
over medium-hot coals (350° to 400°).
  Grill, covered, 10 minutes; turn packets. Open
packets; brush onion slices evenly with remaining
vinegar. Top each slice with 1 tablespoon chutney
mixture. Loosely wrap slices; grill 5 additional
minutes or until onion is glazed and crisp-tender.
Yield: 4 servings.

PER SERVING: 115 CALORIES (5% FROM FAT)
FAT 0.6G (SATURATED FAT 0.1G)
PROTEIN 2.2G   CARBOHYDRATE 27.1G
CHOLESTEROL 0MG   SODIUM 40MG

Roasted Vidalias

ROASTED VIDALIAS

This easy side dish makes a savory accompaniment to grilled fish, poultry, or steak.

4 medium Vidalia or other sweet onions,
     peeled and cut into 8 wedges each
Olive oil-flavored vegetable cooking spray
1 teaspoon dried thyme
½ teaspoon salt
¼ teaspoon freshly ground pepper
1 tablespoon balsamic vinegar
Fresh thyme sprigs (optional)

Arrange onion on a jellyroll pan coated with cooking spray; lightly coat onion with cooking spray. Sprinkle 1 teaspoon thyme, salt, and pepper over onion. Bake at 350° for 30 minutes. Turn onion wedges over; bake 25 additional minutes or until tender.

Spoon onion into a serving dish, and drizzle with vinegar. Garnish with fresh thyme, if desired. Yield: 4 (¾-cup) servings.

PER SERVING: 57 CALORIES (6% FROM FAT)
FAT 0.4G (SATURATED FAT 0.1G)
PROTEIN 1.7G CARBOHYDRATE 12.6G
CHOLESTEROL 0MG SODIUM 297MG

CRANBERRY- AND APRICOT-GLAZED SWEET POTATOES

½ cup water
1⅔ cups chopped dried apricots (about 8 ounces)
¾ cup dried cranberries (about 3 ounces) or sweetened dried cranberries (such as Craisins)
1 (12-ounce) can apricot nectar
1 teaspoon grated orange rind
¼ cup fresh orange juice
2 tablespoons margarine, melted
11 cups (¼-inch-thick) peeled, sliced sweet potato (about 4 pounds)
¼ cup water
Vegetable cooking spray
½ cup firmly packed brown sugar

Combine first 4 ingredients in a saucepan. Bring to a boil, and boil 2 minutes. Remove from heat; cover and let stand 20 minutes. Drain in a colander over a bowl, reserving apricot mixture and cooking liquid. Add orange rind, orange juice, and margarine to cooking liquid; set aside.

Combine sweet potato and ¼ cup water in a 3-quart microwave-safe dish. Cover and microwave at HIGH 18 minutes or until tender, stirring after 9 minutes. Drain well.

Arrange half of sweet potato in a 3-quart baking dish coated with cooking spray; top with half of apricot mixture and ¼ cup sugar. Repeat layers. Pour reserved cooking liquid over sweet potato mixture. Bake, uncovered, at 350° for 30 minutes or until bubbly. Yield: 12 (⅔-cup) servings.

PER SERVING: 263 CALORIES (9% FROM FAT)
FAT 2.5G (SATURATED FAT 0.5G)
PROTEIN 3.0G   CARBOHYDRATE 60.0G
CHOLESTEROL 0MG   SODIUM 57MG

HERB-CRUSTED POTATO WEDGES

2 pounds baking potatoes (about 5 medium)
1 tablespoon olive oil
3 tablespoons grated Parmesan cheese
1 tablespoon chopped fresh oregano
1 tablespoon chopped fresh thyme
2 teaspoons chopped fresh rosemary
¼ teaspoon freshly ground pepper
Olive oil-flavored vegetable cooking spray

Cut each potato into 8 wedges; brush with oil.

Combine cheese and next 4 ingredients in a large zip-top plastic bag. Add potato wedges; seal bag, and shake to coat well. Place potato wedges, skin side down, in a single layer on a 15- x 10- x 1-inch jellyroll pan coated with cooking spray. Bake at 375° for 50 minutes or until tender and lightly browned, turning once. Yield: 8 servings.

PER SERVING: 110 CALORIES (20% FROM FAT)
FAT 2.5G (SATURATED FAT 0.6G)
PROTEIN 3.3G   CARBOHYDRATE 19.2G
CHOLESTEROL 1MG   SODIUM 43MG

BASIL NEW POTATOES

2½ pounds small round red potatoes
2 tablespoons vegetable oil
1½ tablespoons minced garlic
⅓ cup shredded fresh basil
1 teaspoon freshly ground pepper
½ teaspoon salt

Cook potatoes in boiling water to cover 15 to 18 minutes or until tender. Cool to touch; quarter potatoes. Set aside.

Heat oil in a large nonstick skillet over medium-high heat. Add potato and garlic; sauté 5 to 10 minutes or until potato is browned. Sprinkle with basil, pepper, and salt; toss. Yield: 10 (½-cup) servings.

PER SERVING: 111 CALORIES (24% FROM FAT)
FAT 2.9G (SATURATED FAT 0.4G)
PROTEIN 2.6G   CARBOHYDRATE 19.5G
CHOLESTEROL 0MG   SODIUM 125MG

Basil New Potatoes

ROASTED GARLIC MASHED POTATOES

1 whole head garlic
1 tablespoon olive oil
1 pound Yukon Gold or red potatoes, peeled
   and quartered
3 cups water
½ cup low-fat milk
¼ teaspoon salt
¼ teaspoon pepper

Peel outer skin from garlic head, and discard (do not peel or separate cloves). Cut off top one-third of garlic head; rub with oil. Place garlic, cut side up, in center of a piece of heavy-duty aluminum foil. Fold foil over garlic, sealing tightly. Bake at 350° for 1 hour or until garlic is soft. Remove from oven; cool. Remove and discard papery skin from garlic. Squeeze pulp from each clove, or scoop out with a spoon; set pulp aside.

Place potato and water in a saucepan. Bring to a boil; cook 15 minutes or until very tender. Drain. Heat milk in pan over medium heat until hot (do not boil). Add potato, salt, and pepper; beat at medium speed of an electric mixer until smooth. Add garlic pulp; stir well. Yield: 5 (½-cup) servings.

PER SERVING: 105 CALORIES (27% FROM FAT)
FAT 3.1G (SATURATED FAT 0.5G)
PROTEIN 3.9G CARBOHYDRATE 16.6G
CHOLESTEROL 1MG SODIUM 140MG

Roasted Garlic Mashed Potatoes

STUFFED YELLOW SQUASH

4 medium-size yellow squash
Olive oil-flavored vegetable cooking spray
¼ cup chopped green onions
2 tablespoons finely chopped sweet red pepper
2 tablespoons finely chopped green pepper
¾ cup frozen whole-kernel corn, thawed
⅓ cup crumbled feta cheese
¼ teaspoon salt
¼ teaspoon freshly ground pepper
Green onion curl (optional)

Pierce squash several times with a fork. Place squash in microwave oven on paper towels. Microwave, uncovered, at HIGH 4 minutes, rearranging squash after 2 minutes. Let stand 5 minutes.

Cut each squash in half lengthwise; scoop out and discard pulp, leaving ¼-inch-thick shells. Invert squash shells onto paper towels; set aside.

Coat a small nonstick skillet with cooking spray; place over medium-high heat until hot. Add chopped green onions and chopped peppers; sauté until tender. Remove from heat; add corn and next 3 ingredients.

Spoon vegetable mixture evenly into squash shells. Place stuffed shells in a 13- x 9- x 2-inch baking dish coated with cooking spray. Cover with heavy-duty plastic wrap, and vent. Microwave at HIGH 4 to 6 minutes or until thoroughly heated. Place squash on a serving platter. Garnish with a green onion curl, if desired. Yield: 4 servings.

Note: If a 13- x 9- x 2-inch baking dish will not fit in your microwave oven, bake stuffed squash in a conventional oven at 350° for 15 to 20 minutes or until thoroughly heated.

PER SERVING: 88 CALORIES (31% FROM FAT)
FAT 3.0G (SATURATED FAT 1.7G)
PROTEIN 4.2G CARBOHYDRATE 13.7G
CHOLESTEROL 9MG SODIUM 270MG

Stuffed Yellow Squash

ORANGE-STREUSEL ACORN SQUASH

Acorn squash is a winter squash with dark green ribbed skin and orange flesh. It's available year-round but is best from early fall through winter. Other varieties of winter squash include butternut, hubbard, and spaghetti squash.

2 small acorn squash (about ¾ pound each)
¼ cup frozen orange juice concentrate,
     thawed and undiluted
2 tablespoons brown sugar
¼ teaspoon ground allspice
Vegetable cooking spray
⅓ cup corn flake crumbs
1½ tablespoons coarsely chopped pecans
2 teaspoons reduced-calorie margarine, melted

Cut squash in half vertically. Remove and discard seeds. Place squash, cut sides down, in a 13- x 9- x 2-inch baking dish. Add hot water to dish to depth of ½ inch. Bake, uncovered, at 400° for 30 to 40 minutes or until tender. Drain and cool slightly.

Scoop out squash pulp into a bowl, leaving ¼-inch-thick shells. Mash pulp. Add orange juice concentrate, brown sugar, and allspice; stir well. Cut a thin slice off bottom of each squash shell so it will sit flat. Coat baking dish with cooking spray; return squash shells to baking dish. Spoon squash mixture evenly into shells.

Combine corn flake crumbs, pecans, and margarine. Sprinkle crumb mixture evenly over squash. Bake, uncovered, at 400° for 15 to 20 minutes or until thoroughly heated. Yield: 4 servings.

PER SERVING: 155 CALORIES (19% FROM FAT)
FAT 3.3G (SATURATED FAT 0.4G)
PROTEIN 2.3G   CARBOHYDRATE 31.7G
CHOLESTEROL 0MG   SODIUM 113MG

PAN-FRIED DILL TOMATOES

1 cup peeled, diced cucumber (about 1
     medium)
1 tablespoon cider vinegar
¾ cup fine, dry breadcrumbs
3 tablespoons grated Parmesan cheese
2 tablespoons chopped fresh dillweed or
     2 teaspoons dried dillweed
¼ teaspoon freshly ground pepper
⅛ teaspoon salt
2 egg whites, lightly beaten
2 tablespoons water
10 (½-inch-thick) slices tomato (about
     3 medium tomatoes)
Olive oil-flavored vegetable cooking spray

Combine cucumber and vinegar in a small bowl; set aside.

Combine breadcrumbs and next 4 ingredients in a shallow bowl. Combine egg whites and water, stirring well with a wire whisk. Dredge tomato slices in breadcrumb mixture, and dip in egg white mixture. Dredge in breadcrumb mixture again.

Heavily coat a large nonstick skillet with cooking spray. Place skillet over medium-high heat until hot. Add tomato; cook 1 minute on each side or until golden. Serve warm with cucumber mixture. Yield: 5 servings.

PER SERVING: 115 CALORIES (20% FROM FAT)
FAT 2.5G (SATURATED FAT 0.8G)
PROTEIN 5.9G   CARBOHYDRATE 18.6G
CHOLESTEROL 2MG   SODIUM 282MG

Grilled Vegetables with Balsamic Vinaigrette

GRILLED VEGETABLES WITH BALSAMIC VINAIGRETTE

¼ cup balsamic vinegar
2 tablespoons honey
1 tablespoon olive oil
1 teaspoon coarsely ground black pepper
½ teaspoon salt
4 cloves garlic, minced
4 plum tomatoes, halved
2 zucchini, cut lengthwise into ¼-inch
  slices
1 (1-pound) eggplant, cut crosswise into
  1-inch-thick slices
1 sweet red pepper, cut into 8 wedges
1 onion, cut into 2-inch-thick wedges
1 small bunch kale (about 8 ounces)
Vegetable cooking spray

Combine first 6 ingredients; stir well. Combine tomato and next 5 ingredients in a large bowl. Divide vinaigrette and vegetable mixture evenly between two large zip-top plastic bags. Seal; marinate in refrigerator 1 hour, turning bags occasionally.

Coat grill rack with cooking spray; place on grill over medium-hot coals (350° to 400°). Remove vegetables from bags; reserve marinade. Place vegetables on grill rack; grill, uncovered, 7 minutes on each side, turning occasionally and basting with reserved marinade. Yield: 8 (1-cup) servings.

PER SERVING: 87 CALORIES (24% FROM FAT)
FAT 2.3G (SATURATED FAT 0.3G)
PROTEIN 2.7G CARBOHYDRATE 16.6G
CHOLESTEROL 0MG SODIUM 168MG

From left: *Versatile Vinaigrette, Garlic-Blue Cheese Vinaigrette, and Basil Vinaigrette (recipes on page 133)*

DRESSINGS & SALSAS

*A*n exceptional salad dressing transforms simple greens into an extraordinary salad, just as a unique salsa adds flair to grilled chicken or fish. Both create gourmet fare out of everyday ingredients.

Use the dressings on page 131 with the combinations of salad greens described on pages 63 through 65. Drizzle one of the sweeter dressings (pages 132 and 133) over mixed fresh fruit. Or splash a flavored vinegar (pages 134 through 136) over fresh fruit or greens.

For even more culinary excitement, try the salsas beginning on page 136. You can make a salsa with anything from grilled corn to cantaloupe to chiles. Try one as an appetizer with chips, a sauce over meat, a soup topper, a side dish, or a garnish.

Chunky Herbed Blue Cheese Dressing (front) and Zesty Citrus Oil-Free Dressing (recipe on page 132)

Chunky Herbed Blue Cheese Dressing

1 cup nonfat buttermilk
1 cup 1% low-fat cottage cheese
¼ cup reduced-calorie mayonnaise
1 tablespoon white wine vinegar
¼ teaspoon salt
¼ teaspoon ground white pepper
⅓ cup plus 1 tablespoon crumbled blue cheese
2 tablespoons finely chopped fresh basil

Combine first 6 ingredients in container of an electric blender; cover and process until smooth, stopping once to scrape down sides.

Transfer mixture to a small bowl. Stir in blue cheese and basil. Cover and chill at least 2 hours. Serve dressing with salad greens or assorted fresh vegetables. Yield: 2½ cups.

Per Tablespoon: 15 Calories (54% from Fat)
Fat 0.9g (Saturated Fat 0.3g)
Protein 1.2g   Carbohydrate 0.6g
Cholesterol 2mg   Sodium 75mg

Caesar Salad Dressing

2 teaspoons spicy hot mustard
1 teaspoon anchovy paste
1 clove garlic, crushed
½ cup nonfat buttermilk
¼ cup grated Parmesan cheese
2 tablespoons dry white wine
2 tablespoons red wine vinegar
1 tablespoon chopped fresh parsley
1 tablespoon lemon juice
1 tablespoon olive oil

Combine first 3 ingredients in a small bowl; stir well. Add buttermilk and remaining ingredients, stirring with a wire whisk until blended. Cover and chill. Serve over mixed salad greens. Yield: 1 cup.

Per Tablespoon: 19 Calories (62% from Fat)
Fat 1.3g (Saturated Fat 0.4g)
Protein 0.9g   Carbohydrate 0.7g
Cholesterol 1mg   Sodium 80mg

Dijon-Herb Dressing

⅓ cup nonfat mayonnaise
⅓ cup water
¼ cup minced fresh parsley
2 tablespoons rice wine vinegar
1 tablespoon Dijon mustard
½ teaspoon sugar
⅛ teaspoon freshly ground pepper
1 clove garlic, minced

Combine all ingredients in a small bowl, stirring well. Cover and chill thoroughly. Serve with salad greens or fresh raw vegetables. Yield: ¾ cup.

Per Tablespoon: 9 Calories (10% from Fat)
Fat 0.1g (Saturated Fat 0.0g)
Protein 0.0g   Carbohydrate 1.7g
Cholesterol 0mg   Sodium 123mg

Parmesan-Green Peppercorn Dressing

1 cup low-fat buttermilk
¼ cup grated Parmesan cheese
¼ cup nonfat sour cream
¼ cup reduced-calorie mayonnaise
2 tablespoons lemon juice
2 teaspoons dried green peppercorns, crushed
¼ teaspoon pepper
⅛ teaspoon salt

Combine all ingredients in a small bowl, and stir well with a wire whisk. Cover and chill. Serve over mixed salad greens. Yield: 1¾ cups.

Per Tablespoon: 14 Calories (51% from Fat)
Fat 0.8g (Saturated Fat 0.3g)
Protein 0.8g   Carbohydrate 0.9g
Cholesterol 2mg   Sodium 50mg

CREAMY COLESLAW DRESSING

½ cup nonfat mayonnaise
½ cup nonfat sour cream
2 tablespoons sugar
2 tablespoons vinegar
½ teaspoon prepared mustard
¼ teaspoon salt
¼ teaspoon freshly ground pepper

Combine all ingredients in a small bowl; stir until well blended. Cover and chill at least 30 minutes. Toss with your favorite coleslaw ingredients. Yield: 1 cup plus 2 tablespoons.

PER TABLESPOON: 16 CALORIES (0% FROM FAT)
FAT 0.0G (SATURATED FAT 0.0G)
PROTEIN 0.5G CARBOHYDRATE 3.3G
CHOLESTEROL 0MG SODIUM 123MG

Creamy Coleslaw Dressing

CREAMY PESTO DRESSING

½ cup loosely packed fresh basil leaves
½ cup nonfat mayonnaise
¼ cup nonfat sour cream
2 tablespoons pine nuts
2 tablespoons fat-free milk
2 tablespoons white wine vinegar
⅛ teaspoon pepper
2 large cloves garlic, minced

Combine all ingredients in container of an electric blender; cover and process until smooth, stopping once to scrape down sides. Transfer dressing to a small bowl. Cover and chill thoroughly. Serve with salad greens, pasta salad, or grain salad. Yield: 1 cup plus 2 tablespoons.

PER TABLESPOON: 18 CALORIES (50% FROM FAT)
FAT 1.0G (SATURATED FAT 0.2G)
PROTEIN 0.5G CARBOHYDRATE 2.1G
CHOLESTEROL 0MG SODIUM 89MG

ZESTY CITRUS OIL-FREE DRESSING

(pictured on page 130)

2 tablespoons orange zest
½ cup plus 2 tablespoons fresh orange juice
2 tablespoons powdered fruit pectin
2 tablespoons honey
1 teaspoon poppy seeds

Combine all ingredients in a small jar; cover tightly, and shake vigorously. Chill thoroughly. Serve with salad greens, fresh fruit, angel food cake, or grilled fish. Store in refrigerator up to 3 days. Yield: ¾ cup.

PER TABLESPOON: 22 CALORIES (8% FROM FAT)
FAT 0.2G (SATURATED FAT 0.0G)
PROTEIN 0.2G CARBOHYDRATE 5.3G
CHOLESTEROL 0MG SODIUM 0MG

COOL PINEAPPLE DRESSING

½ cup pineapple low-fat yogurt
3 tablespoons frozen pineapple juice
  concentrate, thawed and undiluted
1 tablespoon nonfat mayonnaise
Dash of ground nutmeg

Combine all ingredients in a small bowl, stirring well with a wire whisk. Cover and chill thoroughly. Serve with fresh fruit. Yield: ¾ cup.

PER TABLESPOON: 19 CALORIES (5% FROM FAT)
FAT 0.1G (SATURATED FAT 0.1G)
PROTEIN 0.4G   CARBOHYDRATE 4.0G
CHOLESTEROL 0MG   SODIUM 21MG

CREAMY POPPY SEED DRESSING

½ cup nonfat mayonnaise-type salad dressing
½ cup nonfat sour cream
½ cup unsweetened orange juice
1 tablespoon poppy seeds
1 teaspoon sugar
2 teaspoons lemon juice
⅛ teaspoon pepper

Combine all ingredients in a bowl, stirring with a wire whisk until smooth. Cover and chill thoroughly. Serve with fresh fruit or salad greens. Yield: 1½ cups.

PER TABLESPOON: 12 CALORIES (15% FROM FAT)
FAT 0.2G (SATURATED FAT 0.0G)
PROTEIN 0.4G   CARBOHYDRATE 2.2G
CHOLESTEROL 0MG   SODIUM 50MG

VERSATILE VINAIGRETTE
(pictured on page 128)

¾ cup canned reduced-sodium chicken broth
¼ cup white wine vinegar
2 teaspoons minced garlic
1½ teaspoons olive oil
1 teaspoon Dijon mustard
⅛ teaspoon pepper

Combine all ingredients in a jar; cover. Shake vigorously. Chill. Serve with greens. Yield: 1¼ cups.

PER TABLESPOON: 5 CALORIES (72% FROM FAT)
FAT 0.4G (SATURATED FAT 0.1G)
PROTEIN 0.1G   CARBOHYDRATE 0.1G
CHOLESTEROL 0MG   SODIUM 13MG

BASIL VINAIGRETTE
Omit garlic and mustard. Add 3 tablespoons finely chopped fresh basil and 1 green onion, finely chopped. Yield: 1¼ cups.

PER TABLESPOON: 5 CALORIES (72% FROM FAT)
FAT 0.4G (SATURATED FAT 0.1G)
PROTEIN 0.1G   CARBOHYDRATE 0.1G
CHOLESTEROL 0MG   SODIUM 5MG

GARLIC-BLUE CHEESE VINAIGRETTE
Add ¼ cup crumbled blue cheese and 1 teaspoon sugar. Yield: 1¼ cups.

PER TABLESPOON: 12 CALORIES (68% FROM FAT)
FAT 0.9G (SATURATED FAT 0.4G)
PROTEIN 0.5G   CARBOHYDRATE 0.4G
CHOLESTEROL 1MG   SODIUM 38MG

FYI

Don't be misled by the high percentage of calories from fat in some of these dressings. The total amount of fat and calories is low; it's just that in foods such as dressings, fat makes up a relatively large percent of the calories.

ROASTED YELLOW PEPPER AND BASIL VINAIGRETTE

1 pound sweet yellow peppers, roasted and
    peeled (see page 74 for roasting
    instructions)
⅓ cup white wine vinegar
2 tablespoons extra-virgin olive oil
1½ teaspoons Dijon mustard
½ teaspoon salt
¼ teaspoon sugar
⅛ teaspoon pepper
1 clove garlic, minced
⅓ cup finely chopped fresh basil

    Combine all ingredients except basil in container
of an electric blender; cover and process mixture
until smooth. Stir in basil.
    Serve over salad greens or sliced tomatoes, or use
as a basting sauce or marinade for grilled chicken.
Yield: 1½ cups.

PER TABLESPOON: 16 CALORIES (73% FROM FAT)
FAT 1.3G (SATURATED FAT 0.2G)
PROTEIN 0.2G CARBOHYDRATE 1.2G
CHOLESTEROL 0MG SODIUM 59MG

CHUNKY TOMATO VINAIGRETTE
(pictured on page 2)

1¼ pounds tomatoes, peeled, seeded, and
    finely chopped (about 1½ cups)
¼ cup minced green onions
1 tablespoon chopped fresh basil
1 teaspoon minced fresh thyme
¾ teaspoon minced fresh oregano
¾ teaspoon minced fresh marjoram
⅛ teaspoon freshly ground pepper
3 tablespoons red wine vinegar
2 tablespoons balsamic vinegar
2 tablespoons olive oil
½ teaspoon sugar

    Combine first 7 ingredients in a bowl; toss well.
Combine vinegars, oil, and sugar, stirring well with
a wire whisk. Pour over tomato mixture, and toss
gently. Let stand at room temperature 1 hour.
    Serve with pasta, poultry, or fish; toss with
steamed green beans; or use in marinades for
poultry or vegetable salads. Yield: 2 cups.

PER TABLESPOON: 11 CALORIES (74% FROM FAT)
FAT 0.9G (SATURATED FAT 0.1G)
PROTEIN 0.1G CARBOHYDRATE 0.7G
CHOLESTEROL 0MG SODIUM 1MG

CITRUS VINEGAR

10 (4-inch) strips orange rind
½ medium-size orange, peeled and sectioned
½ small grapefruit, peeled and sectioned
4 cups white wine vinegar

    Combine first 3 ingredients in a wide-mouth
quart glass jar; set aside.
    Pour vinegar into a nonaluminum saucepan;
bring to a boil. Pour hot vinegar over fruit and rind
in jar; cover with lid. Let stand at room temperature two weeks.
    Pour mixture through a wire-mesh strainer
lined with two layers of cheesecloth into decorative
bottles or jars, discarding fruit. Seal bottles with
corks or airtight lids. Use in vinaigrettes and in fruit
or vegetable salads. Yield: 4 cups.

PER TABLESPOON: 2 CALORIES (0% FROM FAT)
FAT 0.0G (SATURATED FAT 0.0G)
PROTEIN 0.0G CARBOHYDRATE 0.0G
CHOLESTEROL 0MG SODIUM 2MG

From left: *Mixed Herb Vinegar, Spiced Vinegar (recipes on page 136), and Citrus Vinegar*

Mixed Herb Vinegar
(pictured on page 135)

½ cup chopped fresh thyme
¼ cup chopped fresh parsley
¼ cup chopped fresh rosemary
¼ cup chopped fresh sage
9 peppercorns
4 green onions, thinly sliced
1 clove garlic, crushed
3¾ cups white wine vinegar
Additional sprigs of fresh thyme, rosemary, or
   sage (optional)

Combine first 7 ingredients in a wide-mouth quart glass jar, and set aside. Pour vinegar into a nonaluminum saucepan; bring to a boil. Pour hot vinegar over herbs in jar; cover with lid. Let stand at room temperature two weeks.

Pour mixture through a wire-mesh strainer lined with two layers of cheesecloth into decorative bottles or jars, discarding herbs. If desired, add additional sprigs of thyme, rosemary, or sage. Seal bottles with corks or airtight lids. Use in vinaigrettes, vegetable salads, soups, or stews. Yield: 3¾ cups.

Per Tablespoon: 2 Calories (0% from Fat)
Fat 0.0g (Saturated Fat 0.0g)
Protein 0.0g Carbohydrate 0.0g
Cholesterol 0mg Sodium 2mg

Spiced Vinegar
(pictured on page 135)

1 tablespoon whole cloves
1 tablespoon whole allspice
1 tablespoon black peppercorns
1 (2-inch) stick cinnamon
1 teaspoon cardamom seeds
1 whole nutmeg, cracked
4 cups red wine vinegar

Combine first 6 ingredients in a wide-mouth quart glass jar, and set aside. Pour vinegar into a nonaluminum saucepan; bring to a boil. Pour hot vinegar over spices in jar; cover with lid. Let stand at room temperature two weeks.

Pour mixture through a wire-mesh strainer lined with two layers of cheesecloth into decorative bottles or jars, discarding spices. Seal bottles with corks or airtight lids. Use in vinaigrettes and in fruit or vegetable salads. Yield: 4 cups.

Per Tablespoon: 3 Calories (0% from Fat)
Fat 0.0g (Saturated Fat 0.0g)
Protein 0.0g Carbohydrate 0.7g
Cholesterol 0mg Sodium 0mg

Black Bean Salsa

2 (15-ounce) cans black beans, drained
½ cup diced sweet red pepper
¼ cup diced purple onion
¼ cup diced cucumber
2 tablespoons diced celery
2 tablespoons minced jalapeño pepper
1 tablespoon chopped fresh basil
2 tablespoons olive oil
2 tablespoons tomato juice
2 tablespoons red wine vinegar
1 tablespoon fresh lemon juice
1½ teaspoons chopped fresh thyme
½ teaspoon ground cumin
½ teaspoon chili powder
¼ teaspoon salt
¼ teaspoon freshly ground pepper
1 clove garlic, pressed

Combine all ingredients in a bowl; stir well. Cover and chill at least 4 hours. Serve with pork or as a dip with no-oil baked tortilla chips. Yield: 3½ cups.

Per Tablespoon: 17 Calories (32% from Fat)
Fat 0.6g (Saturated Fat 0.1g)
Protein 0.8g Carbohydrate 2.3g
Cholesterol 0mg Sodium 36mg

Black Bean Salsa (back) and Two-Tomato Salsa (recipe on page 140)

Grilled Corn Salsa (front) and Papaya Salsa

GRILLED CORN SALSA

This smoky-tasting salsa makes a great salad, too. Just serve it in a mound over torn salad greens.

6 ears fresh corn
1 large sweet red pepper
2 teaspoons vegetable oil
Vegetable cooking spray
½ cup finely chopped purple onion
¼ cup diced California green chile
¼ cup fresh lime juice
1 teaspoon vegetable oil
¼ teaspoon salt
Fresh cilantro sprigs (optional)

Remove and discard husks and silks from corn. Cut red pepper into quarters; remove and discard seeds and membrane. Brush corn and pepper quarters evenly with 2 teaspoons oil.

Coat grill rack with cooking spray; place on grill over medium-hot coals (350° to 400°). Place corn on rack; grill, covered, 20 minutes or until tender, turning every 5 minutes. Cool; cut corn from cob. Place red pepper on rack; grill, covered, 5 minutes on each side. Cool; dice red pepper.

Combine corn, red pepper, onion, and next 4 ingredients in a bowl; stir well. Serve at room temperature with chicken or pork or as a dip with no-oil baked tortilla chips. Garnish with fresh cilantro sprigs, if desired. Yield: 3½ cups.

PER TABLESPOON: 13 CALORIES (28% FROM FAT)
FAT 0.4G (SATURATED FAT 0.1G)
PROTEIN 0.3G CARBOHYDRATE 2.5G
CHOLESTEROL 0MG SODIUM 12MG

A Hot Tip

What's the hottest chile? Generally, the hottest ones have the darkest green skins and pointed tips rather than blunt ones.

SOUTHWEST MELON SALSA

1½ cups diced cantaloupe
1½ cups diced honeydew melon
½ cup chopped green pepper
½ cup chopped purple onion
2 tablespoons chopped fresh cilantro
2 serrano chiles, seeded and chopped
1 clove garlic, minced
3 tablespoons fresh lime juice
1 tablespoon white wine vinegar
1 teaspoon vegetable oil
¼ teaspoon ground cumin

Combine first 7 ingredients in a large bowl; stir well. Combine lime juice and remaining 3 ingredients; stir well with a wire whisk. Pour over melon mixture, and toss gently. Cover and store in refrigerator. Serve with chicken or fish. Yield: 4 cups.

PER TABLESPOON: 4 CALORIES (23% FROM FAT)
FAT 0.1G (SATURATED FAT 0.0G)
PROTEIN 0.1G CARBOHYDRATE 0.8G
CHOLESTEROL 0MG SODIUM 1MG

PAPAYA SALSA

3 cups peeled, seeded, and diced papaya
¾ cup peeled, diced kiwifruit
2 tablespoons chopped sweet red pepper
1½ tablespoons chopped shallot
1½ tablespoons chopped fresh cilantro
1½ tablespoons fresh lime juice
⅛ teaspoon ground allspice

Combine all ingredients in a bowl; toss well. Cover and store in refrigerator. Serve with beef, pork, venison, or fish, or as a dip with baked flour tortilla wedges. Yield: 3½ cups.

PER TABLESPOON: 6 CALORIES (0% FROM FAT)
FAT 0.0G (SATURATED FAT 0.0G)
PROTEIN 0.1G CARBOHYDRATE 1.3G
CHOLESTEROL 0MG SODIUM 0MG

PINEAPPLE-KIWI SALSA

1⅓ cups chopped fresh pineapple
2 tablespoons minced fresh mint
1 tablespoon minced fresh cilantro
1 teaspoon sugar
½ teaspoon ground ginger
1½ teaspoons fresh lemon juice
2 kiwifruit, peeled and chopped
1 jalapeño pepper, seeded and minced

Combine all ingredients in a bowl; stir well. Cover and store in a glass container in refrigerator. Serve with chicken, pork, fish, or low-fat cheese. Yield: 2 cups.

PER TABLESPOON: 12 CALORIES (8% FROM FAT)
FAT 0.1G (SATURATED FAT 0.0G)
PROTEIN 0.1G CARBOHYDRATE 2.9G
CHOLESTEROL 0MG SODIUM 0MG

TWO-TOMATO SALSA

(pictured on page 137)

2 cups diced plum tomato
1 cup diced green tomato
½ cup diced green pepper
¼ cup diced purple onion
1 tablespoon seeded, minced serrano chile
1 tablespoon chopped fresh cilantro
2 tablespoons fresh lime juice
1 tablespoon olive oil
1 teaspoon sugar
½ teaspoon salt
¼ teaspoon coarsely ground pepper
1 clove garlic, minced
Fresh cilantro sprigs (optional)

Combine first 12 ingredients in a bowl; stir well. Cover and chill 3 hours. Serve with chicken or fish or as a dip with no-oil-baked tortilla chips. Garnish with cilantro sprigs, if desired. Yield: 3½ cups.

PER TABLESPOON: 6 CALORIES (45% FROM FAT)
FAT 0.3G (SATURATED FAT 0.0G)
PROTEIN 0.1G CARBOHYDRATE 0.8G
CHOLESTEROL 0MG SODIUM 22MG

GREEN TOMATO SALSA WITH THAI SPICES

4 green tomatoes (about 2 pounds)
1 large purple onion
¼ cup minced fresh cilantro
2 tablespoons fresh lime juice
2 tablespoons fish sauce
1 tablespoon rice vinegar
2 teaspoons seeded, minced serrano chile
2 teaspoons peeled, minced gingerroot
2 teaspoons ground coriander
2 teaspoons vegetable oil
1 teaspoon sesame oil
1 cup chopped green onions
1 cup julienne-sliced sweet yellow pepper

Cut tomatoes and purple onion in half vertically. Cut each half horizontally into thin slices.

Combine cilantro and next 8 ingredients. Add tomato, purple and green onions, and pepper; toss well. Let stand 1 hour. Yield: 16 (½-cup) servings.

Note: Fish sauce is a salty condiment that you can find in Asian markets, specialty shops, and some supermarkets. You may substitute 2 tablespoons Worcestershire sauce, if desired.

PER SERVING: 26 CALORIES (38% FROM FAT)
FAT 1.1G (SATURATED FAT 0.2G)
PROTEIN 0.8G CARBOHYDRATE 4.0G
CHOLESTEROL 0MG SODIUM 264MG

Green Tomato Salsa with Thai Spices

INDEX

METRIC EQUIVALENTS

Metric Equivalents for Different Types of Ingredients

A standard cup measure of a dry or solid ingredient will vary in weight depending on the type of ingredient. A standard cup of liquid is the same volume for any type of liquid. Use the following chart when converting standard cup measures to grams (weight) or milliliters (volume).

Standard Cup	Fine Powder (ex. flour)	Grain (ex. rice)	Granular (ex. sugar)	Liquid Solids (ex. butter)	Liquid (ex. milk)
1	140 g	150 g	190 g	200 g	240 ml
¾	105 g	113 g	143 g	150 g	180 ml
⅔	93 g	100 g	125 g	133 g	160 ml
½	70 g	75 g	95 g	100 g	120 ml
⅓	47 g	50 g	63 g	67 g	80 ml
¼	35 g	38 g	48 g	50 g	60 ml
⅛	18 g	19 g	24 g	25 g	30 ml

Useful Equivalents for Liquid Ingredients by Volume

¼ tsp				=	1 ml
½ tsp				=	2 ml
1 tsp				=	5 ml
3 tsp	=	1 tbls	=	½ fl oz	15 ml
	2 tbls	= ⅛ cup	= 1 fl oz	=	30 ml
	4 tbls	= ¼ cup	= 2 fl oz	=	60 ml
	5⅓ tbls	= ⅓ cup	= 3 fl oz	=	80 ml
	8 tbls	= ½ cup	= 4 fl oz	=	120 ml
	10⅔ tbls	= ⅔ cup	= 5 fl oz	=	160 ml
	12 tbls	= ¾ cup	= 6 fl oz	=	180 ml
	16 tbls	= 1 cup	= 8 fl oz	=	240 ml
	1 pt	= 2 cups	= 16 fl oz	=	480 ml
	1 qt	= 4 cups	= 32 fl oz	=	960 ml
			33 fl oz	= 1000 ml	= 1 l

Useful Equivalents for Dry Ingredients by Weight

(To convert ounces to grams, multiply the number of ounces by 30.)

1 oz	=	1/16 lb	=	30 g
4 oz	=	¼ lb	=	120 g
8 oz	=	½ lb	=	240 g
12 oz	=	¾ lb	=	360 g
16 oz	=	1 lb	=	480 g

Useful Equivalents for Cooking/Oven Temperatures

	Fahrenheit	Celcius	Gas Mark
Freeze Water	32° F	0° C	
Room Temperature	68° F	20° C	
Boil Water	212° F	100° C	
Bake	325° F	160° C	3
	350° F	180° C	4
	375° F	190° C	5
	400° F	200° C	6
	425° F	220° C	7
	450° F	230° C	8
Broil			Grill

Useful Equivalents for Length

(To convert inches to centimeters, multiply the number of inches by 2.5.)

1 in				=	2.5 cm	
6 in	= ½ ft			=	15 cm	
12 in	= 1 ft			=	30 cm	
36 in	= 3 ft	= 1 yd		=	90 cm	
40 in				=	100 cm	= 1 m